Our Stories of Experience, Strength & Hope!

by the

Fellowship of
Recovering
Lutheran
Clergy

*Providing Recovery Support for Lutheran Clergy
Who Suffer from Alcoholism and Other Addictions*

authorHOUSE

*1663 LIBERTY DRIVE, SUITE 200
BLOOMINGTON, INDIANA 47403
(800) 839-8640
WWW.AUTHORHOUSE.COM*

© 2005 by the Fellowship of Recovering Lutheran Clergy.
All Rights Reserved.

No part of this book may be reproduced, stored in a retrieval system, or transmitted by any means without the written permission of the author.

First published by AuthorHouse 12/16/04

ISBN: 1-4184-6507-0 (e)
ISBN: 1-4184-6508-9 (sc)

Printed in the United States of America
Bloomington, Indiana

This book is printed on acid-free paper.

In Remembrance…

This booklet is lovingly and gratefully dedicated to

Pastor Don "Buzz" Busboom

who kept this fellowship nurtured
through its infancy.

We look forward to sharing eternity with you, Buzz, and in the meantime we carry on your work here "…to carry the message to those who still suffer."

*"He was indeed a giant, both in stature and in his love of people. His insight, when counseling, was exceptional. I would marvel over his knowledge of how the alcoholic mind works, so that he could cut through the smoke of self ingratiation and denial to get to the core of an issue. His dedication to establishing what we now know as **The Fellowship of Recovering Lutheran Clergy** enables each of us to realize the fulfillment of what at first was but a dream of reaching out to others with whom we were bound together with our desire to serve as dedicated Pastors despite our common struggle. Each time any one of us connects with another recovering Lutheran Pastor to assist*

or to be assisted in maintaining sobriety, we can remember and honor our brother Don Busboom - better loved by and known by all of us as 'Buzz.' I think if Buzz had been asked to write his epitaph, it would simply read, 'Solo Dei Gloria'."

--Fred G., LCMS Pastor

Table of Contents

Introduction xi

About the FRLC xv

A History of the Fellowship of Recovering Lutheran Clergy 1

Our Stories 15

The Twelve Steps of Alcoholics Anonymous* 95

Step One As Adapted for the FRLC* 97

The Twelve Traditions of Alcoholics Anonymous 98

Only you can decide whether you want to give A.A. a try —whether you think it can help you.* 100

Addiction Assessment 104

Codependency 106

Are You Co-Dependent? 108

Get Help 110

For Bishops, District Presidents and Synod Councils 112

"Nice Sermon, Pastor".. 16
"All my well-intentioned plans for spiritual discipline were turned into "cover stories" (read "lies") for drinking and using."

--Rev. Dave C.

"Everybody drank. It was the Lutheran thing to do." 20
"I figured I was the same kind of drinker as every other pre-minister student."

--Rev. Gary G.

"The disease only progresses and people die from it." 25
"I thought that if I did develop the disease I would notice. I didn't."

--Rev. Mary S.

"Do you remember the keg incident in my story--five more feet and I would have been in a jail just like these guys? That scared me. It occurred then that alcohol could indeed bring me to jail not as a chaplain, but as a resident.".. 28
The truth of what my drinking could do to me scared the daylights out of me at that point.

--Rev. Eric W.

"I knew that I did not want to go back to smoking pot, and not drinking beer was the best way I knew for that." 45

"So, I went to A.A. where I introduced myself as "Chemically dependent" since I just could not bear the thought that I was an alcoholic."

--Pr. Bob L.

"Sitting half stoned in my basement, I gazed at the pipes running along the ceiling and seriously considered suicide." 49

"Fortunately, I am a coward."

--Rev. Henry T.

"How could a popular pastor be an alcoholic?" 51

"The thought would never even have crossed my mind".

--Rev. John W.

"It was with a lot of trepidation and uncertainty that I entered the treatment center in Arizona, and I will never forget the words of the treatment center medical director upon my admission: "I am a recovering alcoholic and a workaholic. Quite frankly, it has been much more of a struggle to deal with my workaholism." 56

"So, I knew I was facing one of the greatest challenges of my life."

--Rev. Elwood R.

"I had always suspected that there was something wrong with me, only I didn't know what it was." 66

I was also terrified that if the church knew who I really was they would want no part of me.

--Rev. Melanie M.

"My creativity led me to believe that I could do anything and deal with any situation." 72

"It was a classic example of grandiosity."

--Rev. Al D.

"I decided to go into treatment. To this day I remember it as the most terrifying, most humiliating, best day of my life." 78

"It was the day my life changed forever."

--Rev. Ed T.

"It continues to amuse me how humans "normalize" the behaviors of the family in which we grow up." 86

". . . my self-esteem was in the cellar, which put me at the mercy of older, seemingly more confident, boys. If I thought a behavior would raise my status, I would do it-- regardless of risk!"

--Pastor Dick W.

Introduction

This book is a collection of personal stories written by ordained clergy from both the Evangelical Lutheran Church in America and the Lutheran Church Missouri Synod. These stories are the personal testimonies of ordained clergy from these two great church bodies who were caught in the hell of alcoholism, other addiction, and codependency and found a way out. Not only did we find recovery, but we found an amazing new way of life that fulfills all the promises of scripture. You can have what we have if you are willing to humble yourself and follow a few simple suggestions.

These stories tell in a general way what it was like, what happened, and what it is like now for us. They are written and shared here in the hopes that other clergy, perhaps you, caught in the same hell as we were, will find hope and deliverance from this disease.

As you read these stories please try to keep an open mind. The diseases of alcoholism, other addictions and codependency are cunning, baffling, and powerful. They are diseases which convince their victims that they don't have this problem. Each one of us was in denial and we had convinced ourselves we did not have this particular problem--that if we could just get certain matters of our life under control we could manage our lives in a more responsible way. But with all the earnestness at our command, with all the prayer and hope we had in God, we could not manage; and our problems only grew worse. What each one of us has in common is that we recognized we were powerless and that we had to have help from someone else. No matter what we tried nothing changed until we said to another human being these difficult words, "I need help."

We are deeply grateful to the program of Alcoholics Anonymous and the many 12-Step programs which have resulted from it. We follow the principles of the 12 Steps and 12 traditions believing these are gifts from a loving God given to help broken people find healing, hope, and new life. We as the FRLC do not offer another way but wholly support these 12-Step groups and insist they are the way to recovery for our particular problems. We had hoped this would not be true for us, but discovered in hindsight what a great gift it turns out to be.

What we offer as a fellowship is supplemental support to clergy and their families who face the unique problem of being clergy in recovery—because it is a profession which does not easily allow for brokenness. We have each struggled with this issue and can offer support and strength.

This book was written by clergy, for clergy. If you are a member of the clergy and you wonder if you may have a problem with alcohol, another addiction, or codependency, we believe it is no accident you are reading these words. Whatever your situation, no matter how much personal, private pain and turmoil your life may be in, we want you to know there is hope. You are not alone. We have each been there. And we have each come through, reclaimed our lives and our ministries and have found a new and amazing life. You can have that life too, but you cannot do it alone. The Good Lord has created us to need each other and for some reason we pastors think we are exempt. We are here to help you and our fellowship, the FRLC, exists for the sole purpose of extending a hand to you. Please read these stories and if you need to talk, call us. We will help you.

There are more than 200 clergy members of the FRLC and we are located in nearly every state. Chances are, there is a pastor somewhere near you who has been through what you are going through and is willing and ready to help you get your life back. We will help you get connected.

We are a completely independent, not affiliated, non-profit organization made up solely of Lutheran clergy recovering from alcoholism, addiction, and codependency. We have no dues or fees and are completely self-supporting through our own contributions. We promise that your anonymity and privacy will be strictly protected.

You may call for help or more information at 800-528-0842. A recovering pastor will answer the phone or you will be given a recorded list of numbers to call for help.

About the FRLC

The Fellowship of Recovering Lutheran Clergy (FRLC) began in 1990 when two pastors, one LCMS, one ELCA, set out to develop a fellowship of Lutheran clergy for recovery from alcoholism. They wanted to provide mutual support and encouragement for those still struggling with this disease. Since then we have grown to over 200 members and several hundred supporting friends.

Today we employ a part-time publicity director, maintain an 800 number hotline (800 528-0842), host annual recovery retreats, hold monthly board meetings, maintain a membership directory (only for those who desire to be available to help others), send out a quarterly newsletter, and maintain a web-site: www.frlc.org. We are also working with ELCA bishops, LCMS district presidents and Lutheran seminaries, offering ourselves as a support and resource to them. We have developed an impaired professionals program as a way for the church to provide help and support to those seeking recovery.

Our membership is open to all Lutheran clergy recovering from alcoholism, other addictions and codependency. Membership is anonymous. Anonymity is expected and respected.

We recognize alcoholism, addiction, and codependency as primary, progressive, predictable, chronic, and terminal. It can, however, be arrested at any stage of its development. Recovery from any and all addiction is a spiritual process. The FRLC bears witness to this truth at every level in the Church.

We are a network of pastors sharing our experience, strength and hope as we recover from alcoholism and other addictions. Our primary purpose is to stay in recovery and help others find it.

"...forgives all my sins and heals all my diseases..." Psalm 103:3

A History of the Fellowship of Recovering Lutheran Clergy

The Beginning

This Fellowship began in 1990 with a series of events that led to the first meetings of recovering alcoholic Lutheran clergy. To the eyes of faith, it would appear that God was working in the lives of several people to plant the vision of bringing this Fellowship to birth.

On the East Coast of the country, a young Lutheran Church Missouri Synod pastor, Rich H., went to treatment for his alcoholism. While in treatment he learned of the existence of the Recovered Alcoholic Clergy Association (RACA) in the Episcopal Church USA and attended a RACA retreat at Notre Dame. He left with a vision of forming a similar organization in the Lutheran Church.

On the West Coast, an ELCA pastor, Melanie M., was celebrating her tenth anniversary of sobriety. She attended the A.A. International Convention in Seattle, Washington, and attended a meeting on clergy in recovery. Excited by the joy she found in meeting other sober pastors and remembering how important a sober LCA pastor had been in her personal recovery, she thought, "What if we had some sort of way to get together as Lutheran pastors in

by the Fellowship of Recovering Lutheran Clergy

recovery which could help carry the message to those who still suffer?"

Rich contacted the Missouri Synod's Task Force on Alcohol and Drug Abuse. They were extremely supportive and the Social Ministry Department of the LCMS in St. Louis began to work with a group of pastors who were interested in alcoholism to write an application for a grant from the Wheatridge Foundation to start the organization.

In the meantime, Melanie spoke to the Division for Ministry about her idea in July of 1990. The ELCA contact thought it was a great idea, but suggested we avoid the bureaucracy of the church and develop an informal network of people in recovery connected by a newsletter. He also thought we should ask <u>Lutheran Partners</u> to publish a story on this new fellowship. (See page 32, by Melanie M.)

Melanie sent out a letter dated August 13, 1990, to all the pastors she knew of in recovery and a few bishops and treatment centers, proposing the idea of developing some sort of "visible organizational presence within the ELCA while maintaining personal anonymity to the extent desired by each individual, in order to: 1) Support to all clergy recovering from addiction, 2) Provide a clear message that the ELCA supports recovery, especially to newly recovering clergy and congregations dealing with clergy in trouble, and 3) Provide a way for newly clean and sober clergy to make contact with others."

She asked recipients to copy her letter and send it to anyone they thought might be interested in and/or eligible for such a network. She received many positive responses to her letter and proceeded to set up an account through the South Western Washington Synod of the ELCA to handle donations made to the newsletter fund. In December 1990 she published the first official newsletter of the LCRN, which stood for "Lutheran Clergy in Recovery Network." The opening page had a welcome column from Melanie, a statement of the purpose and the following article:

"Disguises"

by Rick S.

A basic A.A. tenet is that alcohol is "cunning, baffling and powerful." How true that is! After five months of sobriety I still have days I want to get the old feelings back by drinking. I miss it. Hardly "respectable" for clergy to admit that, but true nonetheless. There is no gain in lying to myself.

But there are other times I am feeling out of sorts or blaming somebody, when I don't recognize that what is really going on is that I simply want to drink. Sometimes

*by the Fellowship of Recovering Lutheran Clergy
we don't even recognize it's working on us. It wears so
many masks.*

*And, in the ministry, it can be so seductively easy
to repress or deny all those feelings. That's why A.A.
members need each other. That's why recovering clergy
need each other. May God's Spirit open the way for scared
addicted clergy to find help and each other!*

One of the people who received that newsletter was Rev. Merrill Kempfert, Executive Director of Parkside Lutheran Hospital, Park Ridge, Illinois, an 88-bed chemical dependence treatment program. Merrill was an LCMS pastor and a member of the Missouri Synod's Task Force on Alcohol and Drug Abuse. He wrote: "Once I received your newsletter, I sent a copy to Richard knowing of his interest in organizing a similar group among the LCMS clergy and to Rev. Dick Krenke, Social Ministry Dept., LCMS, St. Louis."

I received a phone call from Rich H. in January or February 1991 and was elated and astonished to discover how the Holy Spirit had been working among us! Here is my description from issue no. 3 of the LCRN newsletter:

Our Stories of Experience, Strength, & Hope
"God Delegates Task of Forming Network"

Early this year I received the most amazing phone call! It seems that across the country, an LCMS pastor had the same idea of beginning some sort of fellowship, pan-Lutheran, for clergy in recovery. As we spoke, it was almost as if God had taken the task and divided it in half, and assigned one part to me, female, ELCA West Coast clergy; and another to my friend who is male, LCMS and East Coast.

My LCMS friends had been busy doing the organizational stuff to support an initial gathering while I was developing the newsletter and mailing list. They approached the LCMS Board of Social Ministries and Wheatridge about funding the first nationwide event. The planning committee met in Chicago the weekend of April 20 to begin working on this event. I just got off the phone from speaking with Rich, Buzz and Fred, so this is news "hot off the line." We hope to hold our first retreat of the Fellowship of Recovering Lutheran Clergy in the Chicago area during the last week in July or first week of August 1992. It is likely that it will be a Wednesday through Friday event. Our hope is to alternate between Mid-West, West Coast and East Coast locations on an annual basis. The next planning meeting will be October of this year, and I hope to be there. Information has been shared with by the Fellowship of Recovering Lutheran Clergy LCMS District Presidents and the ELCA Conference of Bishops. We hope that Synods and Districts will be able to help with scholarship assistance to the first gathering, so that a minimum of one pastor from each Synod or District would be able to attend.

Statement of Membership--A Working Draft

The Fellowship shall be open to all Lutheran Clergy, regardless of Synodical affiliation and therefore neither endorses nor opposes any particular theological or political stance within the several Lutheran church bodies.

While the Fellowship does not seek an auxiliary relationship with any Lutheran church body, it does, however, seek their endorsement as a viable ministry of healing and spiritual renewal for alcoholic Lutheran clergy.

Membership in the Fellowship is anonymous, and no member may break the anonymity of another.

The Fellowship recognizes alcoholism is a progressive, chronic, and terminal disease which can be arrested in any stage in its development; it is not specifically a moral question. The Fellowship intends to bear witness to this truth at every level in the church.

Wheatridge Foundation awarded the new organization a grant of $10,000 and work began on the first retreat.

Our Stories of Experience, Strength, & Hope

The First Retreat

The first retreat of the Fellowship of Recovering Lutheran Clergy was held at Our Lady of the Lake Retreat Center at the University of St. Mary of the Lake, Mundelein, Illinois. The planning committee consisted of Rich H. (chairman), Melanie M., Buzz, Fred G., Norman Sc., Larry R. and Norm S. (We actually had two "Norms" in the group.) I will confess being nervous about attending the first meeting of the committee as the only ELCA pastor and the only woman in a group of LCMS clergy, but they received me warmly from the very beginning. We asked Dr. Bruce Hartung of the LCMS Ministerial Health office to lead our retreat and Pastor Phil Hansen, author of several small books on alcoholism, to be our retreat chaplain. There were about 22-23 people in attendance and I was the only woman.

The first night of the retreat we sat in a circle. Bruce asked us to introduce ourselves and tell why we were there. This turned into a "First Step" meeting, where we shared our experience, strength and hope. Bruce had anticipated introductions taking 15-30 minutes. We went on sharing until 11:30 at night! He was amazed at the honesty and depth of sharing we had. He had never seen anything like it in a clergy group before.

by the Fellowship of Recovering Lutheran Clergy

The next morning, Bruce led a presentation on time management and self-care. During the break, people were saying things like, "This material is fine--but I could get this at any clergy meeting--it's not what I came here for. This is a unique chance to be with other alcoholics. I want to spend our time learning from and talking with them."

Before lunch the group informed Bruce that our needs didn't fit well into his agenda and we pretty much took it over and turned it into an extended A.A. meeting. There was an instant bond and depth of sharing that was just incredible.

Development of the Fellowship

At the end of the retreat we elected the planning committee to be the first Board of Directors, and instructed them to proceed with the business of developing an organization. The group met several times during the next year to develop a constitution and bylaws and to complete the process of applying for status as a non-profit organization. They planned a second retreat a Mundelien, as it was a central location for most of the members of the Fellowship at the time.

The first board wrestled with the issue of membership. The LCRN had targeted clergy recovering from any addiction, but the group who wrote the grant was

Our Stories of Experience, Strength, & Hope

concerned about "singleness of purpose" in the A.A. tradition and wrote their proposal limiting membership to alcoholics. This view prevailed, at least for the early days of the Fellowship. The decision was made to allow anybody to be on the mailing list for the newsletter, but that retreats would be for alcoholics only. People recovering from other addictions were encouraged to start their own Fellowship.

Other issues arose, including the question of allowing participation of spouses and Lutheran laity who were recovering alcoholics. One of the board members stated that in the fellowship for recovering Roman Catholic priests, the priests stopped coming when they opened the group to the laity. So the decision was reached to limit membership to recovering alcoholic clergy.

The question of membership was debated every year or two for the next ten years or so. We finally realized that the numbers of clergy recovering from other addictions was so small that they would have great difficulty beginning parallel Fellowships. It was hard enough getting THIS one off the ground! We also had some great people who were recovering from other addictions offering to help in much needed ways, and we wanted to be able to use their talents and abilities. By the year 2000, we changed our membership guidelines and elected our first

by the Fellowship of Recovering Lutheran Clergy

non-alchoholic chairman, a recovering ACOA (Adult Child of an Alcoholic), rather than a "pure drunk"!

We sought to publicize the Fellowship through church periodicals as much as possible. <u>Lutheran Partners</u> accepted the story Melanie has included here for publication on June 27, 1991, although the article did not appear for six months. Buzz's story was printed in the <u>Lutheran Reporter</u> and the <u>Lutheran Witness,</u> and we had articles about the Fellowship printed in the <u>Lutheran</u> magazine and <u>Seeds for the Parish</u> as well. Each article generated many letters and a number of new members, but growth was slow. For many years we continued to encounter people who had never heard of the Fellowship.

After several years we decided to work towards beginning regional gatherings of the Fellowship. We decided to begin with the West Coast. The three board members who lived in the Pacific Northwest met and went through the membership directory. The largest concentration of FRLC members was in the Portland area, so they planned a retreat in Portland. The members living in the Portland area decided to meet on a regular basis, and Portland area retreats were offered for the next five or six years.

We had a member of the Fellowship attempt to duplicate this model in the Ohio area, but it never got off the ground.

Our Stories of Experience, Strength, & Hope

As we grew as a Fellowship, we found that it was taking more and more time to keep things going. We hired Buzz as our first Publicity Director. His duties included answering the phone line, keeping the database up to date, and working to publicize the Fellowship in any way possible, including writing articles for church publications. At one point we purchased an ad in Lutheran Partners magazine. We also purchased a commercial display, which Buzz took to several LCMS national conventions and to District and Synodical conventions. Buzz also gave talks about the Fellowship to church groups as the opportunity arose.

At one of the early board meetings, Otto S., a board member, put into language the "magic" of the incredible group dynamics that I have experienced at every gathering of the Fellowship, whether a small group like a board meeting or a larger group like a retreat. He said, *"I finally realized what it is that makes this group so special. We share four languages in common. We all speak the language of "drunkenness." We all speak the language of sobriety in A.A. We all speak the language of "Lutheran." And we all speak the language of "pastor." This is the only place in my life I can use all four languages without having to stop and explain what I mean with one of them."*

by the Fellowship of Recovering Lutheran Clergy

A Time of Struggle, a Time of Growth

From the beginning, the goal of the Fellowship was to be financially self-supporting through our own contributions, but our numbers were small and we relied on the Wheatridge money while it lasted. We generally sent out an appeal letter once a year or so and an offering envelope went out with the brochures; but when the initial grant ran out, we struggled for awhile. Our annual retreat became an occasional retreat, our board members had to pay their own expenses for travel to meetings, and we sought other grant money to keep things afloat.

Aid Association for Lutherans finally gave us a grant for mailings. The Lutheran Church Missouri Synod was a great help in getting us names and addresses of their pastors, but it took a couple years of struggling with the ELCA bureaucracy to get the same information. At first it was decided to target regions where we had significant membership or board members and send an informational mailing with a request for financial support to every pastor three times a year rather than sending a single national mailing. After completing our planned mailings, we realized we had enough money left to do a national mailing. This mailing bore much fruit. Finally, after ten years, people were beginning to recognize our name and be aware that we existed.

Our Stories of Experience, Strength, & Hope

In the summer of 2000 we held a retreat in Minneapolis in conjunction with the A.A. International Convention. A dozen or so members came and people drifted in an out throughout the days, but we regrouped and elected a new board and got things going again.

Buzz's health began to fail around this time and we chose Ed T. to be our new Publicity Director. Ed developed the website and began to use email to communicate to our membership. Our membership base has grown substantially and we are growing closer to our goal of being self-supporting.

The newsletter has been published throughout the existence of the Fellowship. Melanie continued as newsletter editor for a number of years, then Ed took it on for awhile, then Melanie took it back in the fall of 1999. The 800 number has continued, now at Ed's church, and we have updated the brochure and membership directory as needed.

We have begun having annual retreats once again, and in 2003 spouses were invited for the first time.

The publication of this book marks another milestone in the development of the Fellowship. The idea arose from the brainstorming session in Minneapolis, but it took us several years to collect enough stories and to work out the details of publishing it.

by the Fellowship of Recovering Lutheran Clergy

We thank God for the growth and sustenance of this Fellowship and pray that it will continue to be a blessing to pastors struggling with alcoholism, other addictions and codependency, to their families and congregations, and to the church at large for many years to come.

Our Stories

These stories disclose in a general way what our lives used to be like in our ministry struggling with addiction, what happened to change us, and what our lives are like now in recovery. We hope you hear in these stories the pain we lived with and how we were set free from our misery. We hope you hear in these stories that you too can find freedom and a new life.

by the Fellowship of Recovering Lutheran Clergy

"Nice Sermon, Pastor"

"All my well-intentioned plans for spiritual discipline were turned into "cover stories" (read "lies") for drinking and using."

--Rev. Dave C.

"Nice sermon, Pastor."

"What did you say? Oh, thank you. Have a good day."

We've all had this conversation dozens, even hundreds, of times. For me, there was just one important difference. I could not tell this kind person what I had just preached or what the texts of the day had been. Even more frightening was the fact that I had stepped into the pulpit not having done any preparation for preaching. I had not even an idea what the lessons were or what I might say once I stood into the pulpit.

"Came to believe that we were powerless over alcohol; that our lives had become unmanageable."

Unmanageable? No kidding.

We know the old story about pastors working "one hour per week." As my drinking and practice of another addiction got progressively worse, that story became something of a sick joke. Blessed (or perhaps cursed) with the "gift of gab" from my Irish-American heritage, preaching had always come easily to me. I had a school

Our Stories of Experience, Strength, & Hope

background of public speaking, debate, and acting. Like many drunks, my character flaws include insecurity and an overactive need for attention. Perhaps not surprisingly, I found a calling in which I got to be "up front" most of the time, often at the center of the action. Add the chance to stand in for God-- for me, that was an intoxicating as anything poured from a bottle.

Like many others, I made a judgment. Sure, I had a problem; but as long as what happened on Sunday morning came out all right, I was OK. I spent week after week, month after month, "keeping busy" during the week. I was big on church events—meetings, conferences, and committees. I imagined myself much more the scholar than matched my intellectual efforts. I made sure that I scheduled time for "study and reflection" as well as sermon preparation. These blocks of time were easily consumed by drinking. All my well-intentioned plans for spiritual discipline were turned into "cover stories" (read "lies") for drinking and using. Even more insidious was the guilt, shame, and confusion that these failures meant to me. I believed I could fool the congregation (which I did with partial success), but I knew could never fool God. It never occurred to me that I might simply be fooling myself.

"Nice sermon" became like a smoke alarm or Geiger counter for me. As long as I heard it, things were still all

by the Fellowship of Recovering Lutheran Clergy

right. There was only one problem to this plan. Even when the alarms began to go off, I ignored them. My preaching became erratic, sometimes upbeat, at other times, condemning and cold. After a while, it all became a blur.

As best as I can remember, it was autumn when I stepped into the pulpit completely and utterly unprepared. I felt like a complete fraud. "Nice sermon" now seemed a cruel taunt—an accusing finger pointed at the emptiness of my soul. To her credit, my wife asked me, "How can you preach about God's love and forgiveness when you can't accept it for yourself?" It hurt like hell to hear those words, but she was right.

I suffered what I can only describe as a "psychic break" – a sense of complete and utter defeat and desperation a few days later. I told my wife the basics of what I needed. I went into treatment about two weeks later. Ever the "dramatic one," I waited to go into the hospital so that I could speak with the bishop and preach a tear-filled sermon before leaving. I remember one of the treatment center doctors gave me a very hard time about that delay.

I was in the hospital until December. My aftercare plan called for me to go back to the congregation and do "real" work. Even with having to go to 90 meetings in the first 90 days, I found I had plenty of time for ministry and

Our Stories of Experience, Strength, & Hope

recovery with drinking taken out of my days and nights. What a surprise!

My first sermon back on the job was on Christmas Eve. I had received the gift of a new life that year—a life no longer centered on me, no longer ruled by alcohol, and no longer filled with fear and hopelessness. I can't remember what I preached on that night and I'm all right with that. I do recall saying something about God's surprising grace and the willingness to be grateful. Though it was just over 13 years ago, I remember someone said, "Nice sermon. Welcome home, Pastor." It still sounds good to me.

by the Fellowship of Recovering Lutheran Clergy

"Everybody drank. It was the Lutheran thing to do."

"I figured I was the same kind of drinker as every other pre-minister student."

--Rev. Gary G.

My name is Gary. I am an alcoholic. I have been in the ministry for almost 3 decades, but have been sober the last 13 years.

I didn't plan on becoming an alcoholic. I started at the age of 19, and continued with my friends in the synodical system (grades 9 through seminary). Everybody drank. It was the Lutheran thing to do. I figured I was the same kind of drinker as every other pre-ministerial student.

In the parish, it was still the thing to do. Lay people like to take care of preachers and make sure they had plenty to drink. I was adept at wheedling many free drinks, and I knew which people's homes to go to get some. I kept drinking more; but I could afford more, and everybody I drank with drank more.

Then, after 15 years of drinking, my personality changed abruptly. At home I became loud, angry, and out of control. In public I was always a nice, gentle, young pastor. My idea was that I drank and was upset because my family didn't stay in line. At that time I

Our Stories of Experience, Strength, & Hope

buddied with a few neighboring pastors who liked to go out drinking with "lunch" several times a week. We drank most of the lunch.

I evaluated myself to see if I had an addiction (I had had some experience in the field of alcohol treatment). I didn't drink every day or before ministry work; so I took the number of drinks I had in a week, divided it by seven, and came up with an average of three a day. Since the literature said three a day was moderate drinking, I was okay. I just didn't admit that I went without drinking several days a week and just clumped all the drinks together on 2 or 3 days.

During my last move I was careful that nobody could see me drinking or notice. I drank only at home. It increased, my life became more unmanageable, and I finally had enough. I was depressed, had anxiety, was paranoid and had numerous phobias.

I took outpatient treatment and was labeled a high bottom drunk. I discovered A.A. and the 12 Steps. It was scary at first, but then it became the joy of the first time of feeling free and accepted in my life. I took on the family program to treat my "at home personality/anger" and later therapy and treatment for some of my other ills. God took the phobias and paranoia away without my asking, for which I'm daily thankful.

by the Fellowship of Recovering Lutheran Clergy

It changed me spiritually and in my ministry. Spiritually I was not longer hiding from God, but became open and honest with God about everything, just as I was with friends in A.A. I no longer was trying to impress people, but doing those things that the Bible and my ordination vow said I was supposed to do. I became more effective in preaching and could communicate compassion to others. My priorities in ministry have changed, and I'm with another pastor (non-alcoholic) who is compatible to my outlook.

What happened when others knew? The District folks, other clergy, certain lay leaders, and fellow staff members accepted it and didn't hold it against me, as I thought. In fact, I got more respect. I became an advocate for other Lutheran pastors and teachers in the district with drinking problems and have had some wonderful experiences. One man went back drinking and died. He couldn't accept his powerlessness and the sole power of the Triune God.

In A.A. I came across scores of Lutheran lay people from many area churches. They and others accepted me, even though I am clergy. I've had the opportunity to do ministry among alcoholics: baptisms, funerals, weddings, sick calls, and have rejoiced in seeing some alcoholics getting back into

Our Stories of Experience, Strength, & Hope

church - even Lutheran churches! Not my doing, but God's Holy Spirit.

Now that I've been sober this long, I don't care who knows; but I don't deliberately publicize it. I minister to addicted people in my parish, but mostly to their families.

I'm not a senior pastor, and I'm glad. I'm freed up to do almost all pastoral care work, plus shared Word, Sacrament, and teaching. I enjoy the ministry now. I see God guiding and leading me in what I do. I look back and see how God took care of me in ministry through the years and how He worked despite my drinking.

FRLC has made a tremendous impact on me. Other Lutheran clergy had the same problem, the same feelings, the same personalities, and similar experience, strength, and hope. At the first FRLC retreat I went to eight years ago, I even met the same friends I drank with at college and seminary and some of the same pastors I drank with out in the ministry. It was amazing - those 22 years of drinking had been in association with others who enjoyed drinking but had a problem.

My family, others, and the world around me still have problems. I have a different perspective that takes a day at a time and lets God direct all the

by the Fellowship of Recovering Lutheran Clergy

ministry and solve many of the problems, if others turn to Him. A.A. continues to be a big part of my life and so does the joy of serving others in ministry. That's all I have. I'm happy to be sober, and my wish is that you also find peace and happiness.

Our Stories of Experience, Strength, & Hope

"The disease only progresses and people die from it."

"I thought that if I did develop the disease I would notice. I didn't."

--Rev. Mary S.

You'd think that having half of my family (dad, uncles, grandparents, etc.) being alcoholics and drug addicts would teach me. You'd think that being married to an alcoholic who went into recovery at a relatively early age would show me. You'd think eight years in Alanon plus every self-help book on the market at the time would clue me in. But it didn't. I thought that if I did develop the disease, I would notice. I didn't.

In preparation for going to seminary, I needed to finish, at age 35, my bachelor's degree; so I went to a local university. With homework added to dealing with three small kids at home, I no longer had time for Alanon; and I slowly stopped working any kind of a program. I don't think that fact, added to the extra stress, made it a coincidence that I began to drink a bit more--just to relax.

Since I didn't drink at parties (I talk too much when I drink, it's embarrassing) and I didn't drink and drive, alcohol didn't seem to be causing me any problems. But when my husband noticed during my first year at seminary

by the Fellowship of Recovering Lutheran Clergy

that "a lot" of wine bottles were in the trash and voiced his concern, I had to listen. I had been attending A.A. as a visitor, to keep him company, and get out of the house as a break from school work for a couple of years. Even when one thinks they don't have a drinking problem, A.A. can "ruin their drinking."

Not fully convinced of my own problem, I stopped drinking for a while, just to see what it was like. Then I had a couple of those drunk dreams, where you wake up after having a drink in your dream, in a cold sweat, ashamed and afraid. I told my husband about them, and he said, "Honey, a lot of us have those." I didn't want to be one of "us," but I didn't want to lose all the wonderful things in my life either. I had hung around the program long enough to believe that the disease only progresses and people die from it.

So I began working the program in earnest--most of the time. I got a sponsor, began the Steps, and stopped drinking. I haven't found it necessary to have any alcohol in almost seven years. I did have an "accident" once. Someone told me the glass I had picked up was cranberry juice. One swallow told me different. The reaction my body had to the one, unintended sip of wine was so very weird! I was newly convinced that alcohol is not my body's friend--nor my spirit's.

Our Stories of Experience, Strength, & Hope

God be praised, I had friends around me who kept an eye out for how I was doing for the next couple of hours, and the mistake didn't trigger a slip. But I can't pretend, at least not today, that I can drink like a normal person.

It is a little odd to be clergy with this problem. But I run into others, Lutheran and other folks, when I am least looking for them. I finally told my bishop, two years into my first call. He is supportive and kind and knows I am available to other female clergy who may need to talk about this. It is not my overriding issue in life anymore, just a part of who I am. Now if only there were 12 Steps towards preaching which moves mountains!

by the Fellowship of Recovering Lutheran Clergy

"Do you remember the keg incident in my story--five more feet and I would have been in a jail just like these guys? That scared me. It occurred then that alcohol could indeed bring me to jail not as a chaplain, but as a resident."

The truth of what my drinking could do to me scared the daylights out of me at that point.

--Rev. Eric W.

Roughly four years ago, I discovered grace and freedom not in a church, not in the word and sacrament understanding of grace in my denomination, but in the rooms of Alcoholics Anonymous and a jail. The day I started to go those rooms, I began to grow up. My life went from being lived as my will to being lived as God's will. And my call to being a pastor was transformed and changed.

I have been asked to write my story for this book as a service to those pastors and seminarians who still suffer from alcohol and other addictions. I thank Jesus for his

Our Stories of Experience, Strength, & Hope

permission to write my story for this publication. In the past I would have wanted to draw attention to myself, to have you read it and feel good about me. But as I write this today, after prayer and discernment, I really do write this because of the alcoholic who still suffers may benefit from reading it.

Some of my story, well actually quite a lot of it, revolves around call to ministry and seminary. That's where I finally admitted that I was an alcoholic; and it changed my approach about wanting to be a pastor, my theology, and my pastoring style.

I was a namby-pamby type person as pastor. Now I always pray that I speak in a bluntness that is still heard as the compassion it is meant to be. This story may not be your story. Some of what you read here may not apply to you. If that is the case, then stop reading my story and read another story in this book. Alcohol has all sorts of ways of getting its hooks into us. If you're an alcoholic, I pray that some part of this book will help you find the healing that you need and it doesn't have to be my story. It may very well be another. Read that one and get the help you need.

This story may seem long to you. Some pastors tend to be longwinded. We like to hear the sound of own voice. We think we have something important to say. Maybe you agree, maybe you don't. I also know for sure that as an alcoholic, I love to talk about myself, particularly in a way

by the Fellowship of Recovering Lutheran Clergy

that makes me look good. In that manner, I am a person of the lie. I need to work my program which means I am both saint and sinner and not just one or the other. I will endeavor to make this short so that I can continue to work my program of not being the center of God's universe and continue my life as me, as God intended me to be.

I grew up in Pennsylvania in a very safe, stable home. If I had any complaints (and for a long time, I took every opportunity to make my complaints[1]) it was that my upbringing was too safe. Mom wouldn't allow me to go out for rough sports like football. I tried to convince her to let me be on the wrestling team in junior high, but after two years she refused to sign the permission papers. She was concerned for my health and safety. Today I thank her for loving me the best she knew how.

She did and does a fine job. But back then, I hated her for it. I saw her as trying to raise me to be a wimp. I saw myself as weak when compared to my friends who got to go out for the rougher sports, the heavy hitting, the proving ground of adolescence. I felt like my legs were cut off.

---

[1] As alcoholics we do that a lot. I am talking about complaining. We complain profusely and creatively about bishops, synod events, our churches, our parishioners, our families, and our friends. And it usually comes in the form of gossip.

Our Stories of Experience, Strength, & Hope

I really felt a barrier between my friends and me. I used alcohol to bridge that gap.[2]

As I reached senior high, my friends started to host beer parties. And it wasn't just beer at the parties either. Hard liquor and marijuana abounded. The night before one Mother's Day, I went to party with the mission of proving to my friends that I knew how to get to drunk. I poured myself a glass of vodka, not a shot glass but a regular drinking glass. I succeeded in my mission. I was so drunk, I actually blacked out. A black out is when someone drinks so much he loses awareness of what he is, and he does not remember it the next day. They are hot excuses for bad behavior, i.e., I was so drunk I didn't know what I was doing. THEY ARE REAL. THAT THEY ARE REAL IS WHAT MAKES THEM SO DANGEROUS. The one having them is unaware that his or her activities can hurt another, i.e., drunk driving.

One thing I do remember from that night was that I tried to lick the leg of the president of my junior class. She and her brother, a senior, were actually quite forgiving. Apparently he could get just as messed up as I, and she had been around guys who got just as messed up as I. For

---

[2] I am however convinced that had my mother let me go out for sports I still would have found alcohol.

by the Fellowship of Recovering Lutheran Clergy

everyone at the party, including me, it was clear that I needed to go home. And so I did--drunk.

I remember telling my mother that no, I hadn't been drinking. She told me I had and told me to go to bed. She put the red bucket, the one we used when we had stomach flu, next to the bed. I showed her. When I had to throw up the next day, I made it to the toilet. Our bathroom had a door that opened into my parents' bedroom, so she got to hear it all. Happy Mother's Day! Needless to say, we didn't go to church that morning, mostly because of shame on all family members' parts. My opinion was that I pretty much ruined that year's Mother's Day.

Interestingly enough, I was able to cool it, that is, stifle my drinking until I left for college. The rest of high school was mostly miserable, although I joined the stage crew for our high school's theatrical productions and smoked pot every now and then. When I graduated from I high school, I didn't stick around after the ceremony to say good-bye to any friends. I literally didn't know whom to call a friend. I made it home 30 minutes before my parents did. They had the family over to celebrate my graduation. My friends were drinking at their parties where their parents left them alone. Parents shouldn't do that, but at that time I hated my parents for not being the kind who could look the other way. Alcoholics hate what is good for them.

Our Stories of Experience, Strength, & Hope

Then it was off to college and FREEDOM! Really, at least I thought it was going to be freedom. Free to drink alcohol and smoke pot and keep the grades respectable so as to not arouse suspicion with the folks back home. I was actually able to do that. I joined a fraternity, the drug house fraternity. I learned that five years after I graduated from college, my fraternity had its charter revoked by its national office because the president at the time was caught by the police selling drugs. What more can be said about this time? I remember a toga party, after losing my toga, totally drunk and stoned running around the house in my underwear at a party. Beer and pot tended to make me physically unattractive. I was quite a sight.

And I was a puker. I was very good at the gentleman's puke, where I would stand over the toilet instead kneeling next to it. I remember after a heavy night of drinking I was interviewing for a newspaper internship and having to swallow back some bile I coughed up inside my mouth. I had the hangover sweats. I had to have looked terrible. You know what? I got the internship! But when I learned the hours would include Saturdays, I didn't take it because I wanted to party on Saturdays.

I was also incredibly misogynistic, too; that is, I was mean to women. Alcohol didn't make me that way but, boy, did that behavior come out when I drank. Something deep down inside made me realize behaving in such a

by the Fellowship of Recovering Lutheran Clergy

manner was evil. I felt shame and wanted to stop. My senior year in college I believed my bad behavior was due to my drinking and actually decided to stop drinking. That lasted three days. On the third day, we had a party at the frat house and I again was making crude sexual jokes and advances toward the women who came to our parties. Now my fraternity brothers and I were not great catches. We were the kind of guys decent mothers and fathers warn their sons and daughters about. We tended to attract women who did not have a lot of respect for themselves. They did have enough respect to reject me. I realized at that point that I didn't need alcohol to act like a jerk; I could do it sober, and so I believed alcohol was not my problem. And thus I went back to drinking. Ah, freedom.

There is one other incident from college that bears repeating. My fraternity house had a flat roof. One night during a party, we had a keg on the roof of the house. After midnight, when the keg was empty, I pushed it off the roof without looking below. It landed five feet away from someone who had passed out on the ground outside our house. Another five feet and the person's head would have been smashed and I would have gone to jail.

While yet in college I attended the local Lutheran campus ministry program. I would barely go on a regular basis due to being hung over on Sunday mornings, but they usually served a hot lunch after worship and that would

Our Stories of Experience, Strength, & Hope

draw me out. One time for worship they had a speaker from the Lutheran Volunteer Corps (LVC) come and give a recruitment talk. The Lutheran Volunteer Corps is a year-long commitment of working at service oriented ministry in the inner city of an American city, living on a stipend and living with other people in community. I don't know why I signed up, but I did.

My first year in LVC I discovered one of my housemates was a recovering alcoholic. She was starting Alcoholics Anonymous that year; and when we sat as a house to discuss how we as a community of volunteers would live together that year, she asked that we neither keep alcohol in the house nor throw parties with alcohol. We agreed to that, but we got a small refrigerator, 3 feet by 3 feet, for beer, without asking her how she felt about it. Even so, for some reason I felt a need to respect her needs and minimized my drinking. Later in recovery I realized that I could be pretty stubborn and not drink but that didn't mean the quality of my life improved. Remember, I could be jerk without alcohol. I learned that in college.

That year in LVC I suffered from severe depression. I had insomnia, nightmares, high anxiety of emotions (alcohol had shut my emotions off). At one point in the year I wanted to jump off the porch roof of our house, so I went up on the roof, hoping to draw attention to myself. When I realized I wasn't getting any attention, I got back

by the Fellowship of Recovering Lutheran Clergy

inside and was sitting in my room shaking. I walked into the room of the recovering alcoholic and admitted that I had wanted to jump off of the roof. She called the emergency hotline for the psychiatric services. They prescribed Zoloft, an anti-depressant, over the phone and set up an appointment for me to go see a counselor the next day. That weekend I went to party and drank while on the anti-depressants, even though the directions with Zoloft said not to drink. As I look back now I see that without alcohol I was depressed. Alcohol protected me from feeling my emotions. Without alcohol, I didn't know how to feel or live.

I did two years in LVC feeling very depressed. Following my second year in LVC, I went to work at a Catholic service camp in West Virginia for two years. The staff loved to drink together and I fit right in. Funny thing my depression lifted during those two years. FREEDOM! At least I thought I was free because my depression lifted. Actually the alcohol helped stifle emotions that I didn't know how to handle.

Now somehow, after those four years of doing volunteer service work in the inner city and rural areas, I heard a call from God to be a pastor, both the inner call and the outer call. What was God thinking? Actually I thought the church had a lot of problems like hypocrisy so

Our Stories of Experience, Strength, & Hope

maybe I could fix it. EEK! Anyway, I decided to follow God; but I kept drinking.

My seminary candidacy interviews drew up only two glaring issues: how I handled anger and that I made generalizing comments. I am still not sure what they meant by the latter, but I understood well enough what they meant by the former. I had yet to learn how to express anger in a healthy manner. They recommended counseling while I was in seminary, which I did. But neither they nor the interviewing psychologist detected any hint of alcoholism. It's a deceptive disease that even those who have it don't know it.

Seminary was a strange drinking environment. My seminary had social events that served alcohol. After all, didn't Martin Luther have the tables cleared of books and paper at the end of each day to make way for food, drink, and music? Then again, I asked myself, just how much drinking do I want to do in front of everyone else? As much as I can drink without other people knowing! I didn't often let others see me get drunk. I had some interesting experiences in swapping drinking stories with friends at seminary as well. Once my wife (we met at seminary and got married within a year) and I had dinner with another seminary couple and the dinner conversation turned to people swapping funny drinking stories. The other three did have funny ones, but none of mine

by the Fellowship of Recovering Lutheran Clergy

produced any laughter. Instead, they created awkward silence.

I wrote the majority of papers the first two years of seminary while I was drinking. I tried to write what I thought my professors wanted to hear and I got B's. At that time I was also starting to 'manage' my drinking and driving. But then came the Clinical Pastoral Education summer, the CPE.

It was interesting that my whole second year I had been interviewing and applying to various CPE programs and was coming up empty. One particular interview I wore jeans. That is just plain stupid and no-no for CPE interviewing. I should have known better; and when the interviewer called me on it, I copped an attitude. None of my interviews went exceedingly well. I needed a CPE experience before internship.

While taking a class on urban ministry, we had a chance to visit a jail. The chaplain giving the tour talked about his desire to have student chaplains for a summer program. I asked if that would include a CPE. He said yes and under special circumstances I was able to do my CPE at the jail. FREEDOM! Actually freedom was coming. Not the freedom I thought, but freedom I actually needed.

That summer my wife was away at her CPE site, two states away. My first week of jail ministry was eye opening. I felt like I was five years old. I drank a little

Our Stories of Experience, Strength, & Hope

each night at home. By the end of the week, I was drinking quite a bit. My wife called once and I remember little of the conversation. I felt badly about that; and when I returned the following week to my CPE site, I had my first one-to-one meeting with my supervisor. When he asked what I thought, I ended up talking about how inadequate I felt, crying in a self-pitying way and then confessing about my drinking all the week before. He looked out the window onto the courtyard and said thoughtfully, "If you come here drunk or hung over, your CPE here is over. My suggestion is that you visit the program dorm of the jail where they have addictions treatment and 12-Step meetings. I also suggest that you talk with some other chaplains who are a part of Alcoholic Anonymous."

I wanted to be pastor and CPE was a prerequisite, so I did what he said. Now, I don't like doing what other people suggest and I don't like having anything hung over my head; but for whatever reason, God most likely, I took his advice and my life changed.

The program dorm of the jail consisted of men who for various reasons wanted help with their addictions. Their motivations are not important to my story; after all, I initially went there because it was strongly suggested to me. In those rooms and halls I heard the men who were incarcerated telling my story. In some way, if the men were telling the truth about what they did, I was no

by the Fellowship of Recovering Lutheran Clergy

different in my drinking and why I drank and my reckless behavior while drinking. You remember the keg incident in my story--five more feet and I would have been in a jail just like these guys? That scared me. It occurred then that alcohol could indeed bring me to jail not as a chaplain, but as a resident. The truth of what my drinking could do to me scared the daylights out of me at that point.

The gospel became clear to me as I began talking to other chaplains who were in Alcoholics Anonymous. One of them was a Lutheran, a member not only of A.A. but also of the Fellowship of Recovering Lutheran Clergy (FRLC). I don't know if he'll write his story for this book. I will say his story and mine are very different. But our stories were not different in how and why we were alcoholics. And aside from A.A. he would always say, "How could God call me [himself] to be a pastor?" Until internship I didn't understand what he meant by that. I'll say more about that later.

I still had my doubts about whether or not I was an alcoholic. I wasn't drunk all the time. I had never lost a job or my wife or my family or my friends. Here, though, I realized something early. I never had a job beyond a volunteer stipend or summer work! And even my CPE could have been lost if I came in drunk or hung over. I had no friends that I kept in touch with from high school or college. And later, after I started going to meetings, working with a sponsor and working on the 12 Steps, my relationship with my wife and family improved immensely. (I never saw there was anything wrong with it before, which was a lack of empathy on my part.)

Another chaplain, actually a fellow student in CPE with me, simply suggested that if I questioned if I was alcoholic that I give Alcoholics Anonymous three months of meetings and that should help me decide. Starting on internship that fall, I took her advice. Two months later, I got a sponsor who is also part of FRLC. We began the Step work. What a year. At times I didn't know who I was anymore. I wasn't using alcohol to stifle my feelings anymore. With A.A. and my sponsor I was slowly piecing together a new way of living. That was key in order for me to stay sober. I remember early in a meeting I heard one guy with 12 years of sobriety say that he was stubborn enough to stop drinking for a time, but that did not mean his life was any better, in fact it was worse. I related to that. I could just stop drinking; but I needed something healthy to replace the drinking. That something is someone and that someone is Jesus. A.A. helped make that concrete in a way that the church did not.

I really appreciate the fact that on internship I started my recovery because just as interns are beginning to establish their patterns, I could learn a pattern of health and gratitude. We preach in pulpits about gratitude but the

by the Fellowship of Recovering Lutheran Clergy

alcoholic mind may not see a lot to be thankful for in the church. My recovery was teaching me to pay attention to what was good and let go of what was not so good in the church. That helped me a great deal. One night I came from an A.A. meeting where the topic was "What are we thankful for that we have received from our program?" As I drove home from that meeting, I recalled the pastor who always asked how could God called him to be pastor. It hit me then: he didn't say that as a question but as statement of gratitude. God called him as God has called me as sheer gift of grace to serve as a pastor. I return to that piece of wisdom on a daily basis.

My final year of seminary was bit rocky at the beginning. I never thought there was a lot of alcohol at my seminary until I wasn't drinking any of it. There was always a lot of drinking at seminary; it just didn't seem like a lot to me until I stopped. At the apartments a friend came over to visit and brought a gin and tonic with him. Well, that was okay. I wouldn't have alcohol for him and my drinking problem was my problem, not his. Then I visited him at his apartment where a bunch of people were drinking and after little bit I needed to leave. In early recovery I felt uncomfortable around people drinking and the easy and real solution at the time was to excuse myself. And that was okay. But I needed to continue to work my program.

Our Stories of Experience, Strength, & Hope

My next sponsor was not a pastor and that was a very good move for my recovery. I don't ask pastors to be my sponsor anymore. We the clergy in recovery have lot to learn from lay folk in recovery. Because of boundary issues I do not pick church members to be my sponsor, but always look for a non-clergy person. We reworked the Steps. I also hooked up with other seminarians who were in recovery. We even started an A.A, meeting at the seminary.

I am a different person today. Saint and sinner means a lot to me. My disease and recovery are constant reminders of who I truly am. God gives me the grace to see others as they are. The church has its antagonists of which I am one. The church sometimes has priorities that I believe need to be replaced with greater priorities. But instead of getting angry and staying angry and drinking a poison called resentment, I can respond to the needs and opportunities of the day and help my church to stay focused and healthy in it mission to its community. I was not going to get any of those gifts if I had not gotten into A.A. recovery.

At times I have given up responsibility for getting to meetings saying that my schedule is just too busy. I haven't had an alcoholic slip, but the old me comes back at times. I'm learning now, on what is my 4th anniversary of recovery, that as always my program and my meetings for A.A. come first, regardless of what the church needs

by the Fellowship of Recovering Lutheran Clergy

or offers. I don't lose sleep over ministry and I trust God's presence in it.

Someday I want to do more jail ministry or better yet, create a church on the outside with the men and women who have been residents in our country's detention facilities and are in recovery. The men I heard from that summer didn't know it, but they were helping me realize that I had a problem with drinking. Their gift to me was a strong dose of reality, of what my reality could be. Maybe some of them are still in jail and not in recovery. But their stories helped me in ways I did not see coming. FREEDOM! Freedom to admit my sins; freedom to ask for forgiveness; freedom to make amends; freedom to learn from the past; freedom to look forward to the future; freedom to enjoy and live in the present; freedom from being hung over or coming out of a blackout; freedom of more money in my pockets; freedom to feel my emotions but not be owned by them; freedom for closer, more intimate relationships with my wife, family and friends; freedom to be alive to God and dead to alcohol.

If you think you have problem with alcohol, I say to you, give it three months. Your collar doesn't make you Superman and your drinking doesn't make you the Devil. And help is a phone call away.

Our Stories of Experience, Strength, & Hope

"I knew that I did not want to go back to smoking pot, and not drinking beer was the best way I knew for that."

"So, I went to A.A. where I introduced myself as "Chemically dependent" since I just could not bear the thought that I was an alcoholic."

--*Pr. Bob L.*

I got into recovery during my second year of seminary. I had spent my first year having a great time, drinking beer and smoking pot. Of course, that did not make me the best of students. I struggled with New Testament Greek and withdrew failing from Hebrew. Much of what was happening in the classrooms that year was a mystery to me.

Over the summer a friend decided she was drinking too much and checked herself into a treatment center. She invited me along as a concerned person. One of the conditions was that I not drink or use for the 30 days she was going to be in her program. My last drink was on July 4, 1986, with a clear intention to return to drinking and using in 30 days. After a week or so, the staff suggested

by the Fellowship of Recovering Lutheran Clergy

that I take a look at my own drinking and using (surprise!). I have been clean and sober since.

I checked myself into a treatment program about a mile away from seminary. After classes began that Fall I attended their Aftercare program. They suggested that I go to A.A., so I did. I knew that I did not want to back to smoking pot, and not drinking beer was the best way I knew for that. So, I went to A.A. where I introduced myself as "Chemically Dependent" since I just could not bear the thought that I was an alcoholic. But one thing became abundantly clear: I was staying clean and sober. My second year of seminary produced problems again with Hebrew; and as a result, I was on academic probation for two quarters.

The treatment center suggested I find a sponsor, so I did. He had 14 years of recovery when I had less than 14 weeks. He went to two meetings a week and was very comfortable with himself and his recovery. I wanted what he had. We spent many long hours over "coffee," which often was an ice cream sundae.

Next came internship. With less than a year of recovery I went to a large congregation in a small town. I felt as if my recovery was on display. I had, of course, told my supervisor of my being in the program. He in turn told the other pastor who in turn told his wife! So much for anonymity! I began attending new A.A. meetings, which

Our Stories of Experience, Strength, & Hope

they were not doing right. I discovered that it was difficult to speak as Bob the recovering person rather than Bob the new pastor in town. So, I went down the road to a larger town where I could remain anonymous.

While I was on internship, someone mentioned at a meeting that they never considered themselves to be an agnostic until they read chapter four in the Big Book. So, of course, I had to read chapter four since I had skipped over it. After all, I was becoming a Lutheran pastor. How could I be an agnostic?

I discovered that I was the sort of agnostic that believed in God but had great doubts about God believing in me. I also discovered that I had in fact used the "substitution" method for Step 2. I had relied on A.A. and the groups to restore me to sanity. Now in the wilderness of Iowa it was time to come to believe that God could restore me.

Then I went back to seminary again and to my old meetings. Again I could spend time with my sponsor. I finished my course work early, so I spent my last quarter reading and studying the history of A.A. and the Oxford groups. Following my graduation from seminary, I completed a one-year CPE residency at Hazelden. I completed my third, fourth, and fifth Steps and felt ready for parish ministry at last.

by the Fellowship of Recovering Lutheran Clergy

And again, I was off to an even smaller town, one with two very small congregations. There were several in the congregation who recognized my "Easy Does It" bumper sticker for what it was. And again, attending meetings in the town in which I lived was too difficult to sort out "Bob the alcoholic" from "Pastor Bob."

Our Stories of Experience, Strength, & Hope

"Sitting half stoned in my basement, I gazed at the pipes running along the ceiling and seriously considered suicide."

"Fortunately, I am a coward."
--Rev. Henry T.

Like a tide coming in, a heavy drinker gradually finds him(her)self caught in bigger and bigger waves of alcoholic compulsive escapism. I knew I was in deep trouble, yet no resolves or promises to myself availed anything. I still needed that next drink.

I was depressed and angry at myself. Sitting half stoned in my basement, I gazed at the pipes running along the ceiling and seriously considered suicide. Fortunately, I am a coward.

My wife and two of our closest friends did an intervention which was supported by our bishop. Instead of threats and scolding, he put me on a plane that same afternoon to be admitted to a hospital supported by our denomination. I was frightened and ashamed but grateful that my disease was recognized, and I was entered into a treatment program. Self help was out of the question. I

by the Fellowship of Recovering Lutheran Clergy

knew very well that I was powerless over alcohol. The games were over.

That was 19 years ago. Sobriety works.

Our Stories of Experience, Strength, & Hope

"How could a popular pastor be an alcoholic?"

"The thought would never even have crossed my mind".
--Rev. John W.

I often called myself a sophisticated drunk. It was a phrase I would use often in my early days of sobriety. My alcoholism progressed slowly. Unlike others, I didn't have my first drink until I was 21. I quickly made up for it during my senior year in college and as I began seminary. I drank to celebrate. I drank because I enjoyed the taste. I drank to drown my problems. It seemed so normal back in those days.

My drinking continued to be quite sophisticated in my first parish. I had my social cocktails when out to dinner and drank to unwind after meetings and on Sunday afternoons after church. As I think back on it, this was also a time I began to drink to drown problems and concerns in my congregation and in my life.

My second congregation was a party congregation and my drinking increased but I always thought I could handle it. I'm sure it was somewhere during these years that my wife began to show concern about my excessive drinking. But I always knew better. I was respected and loved by my congregation, friends, and peers. How could a popular

by the Fellowship of Recovering Lutheran Clergy

pastor be an alcoholic? The thought would never even have crossed my mind.

A hope my wife had when I accepted the call to my third congregation was that this would lead me to "cut down." In this congregation, though, I had a partner who could more than keep up with me. I drank to celebrate, but I increasingly drank when depressed about my declining congregation and my personal concerns.

My home was a "safe" and "protected" place where I could drink without consequences. I also had a wife who would protect me and my reputation. As problems in my parish increased, I was beginning to think that I might actually have a problem. When my daughter gave me a book on how to stop drinking without A.A., I began taking inventory of myself and my drinking patterns. I began to make plans to cut down and only drink when I was out to dinner. I changed brands. I would move from gin to whiskey to bourbon to beer to wine, always ending in failure and a significant drunk.

During this time period I had a number of periods of sobriety or "dry drunks." But I soon made up for these times when I resumed my drinking. One day, probably when I was drinking to unwind, I read about the Fellowship of Recovering Lutheran clergy and saw the 800 number in a church publication. By God's grace I called it and heard the voice of an empathetic pastor, a fellow

Our Stories of Experience, Strength, & Hope

drunk, who told me that there was hope for recovery. *We* talked a lot about A.A. and he promised to send me some support and stay in touch.

A few days later I received the A.A. Big Book and a phone call from a classmate who was also in recovery and part of this organization. I wish I could say my drinking ended at that time. But my pride told me I could still stop drinking without A.A.. During this time I saw a therapist who had no understanding of alcoholism and was, as I later on found out, probably an alcoholic himself. I also took some inventory of myself and received some inspiration through the admission, recovery, and death of my boyhood hero Mickey Mantle. I was actually able to stop at this time for about six months. But a new crisis in my congregation developed, and I resumed my drinking career with considerably less sophistication.

I don't know if I had reached bottom, but I definitely saw the bottom when, after a two- day binge, I decided to go to my first A.A. meeting. Scared and hung over, I walked though the door that by God's grace would change my life. I discovered at this meeting that alcoholics were people--many different people--whose stories of failure and hope gave me inspiration to quit for good. I now began to realize what my FRLC supporters were talking about when they spoke so highly about A.A.. My A.A. meeting actually became the support group I never really had at

by the Fellowship of Recovering Lutheran Clergy

that time in my congregation. They accepted me not as a pastor but as a fellow drunk trying to stay sober one day at a time.

Early in my sobriety I received a call to my present congregation; and by God's grace, I accepted that call and entered my new parish sober. One of the first things I did in my new congregation was to seek out new A.A. meetings which I continue to attend.

In my conversations with my fellow members of FRLC, I was often encouraged by their stories to be open about my alcoholism in my congregation. I would always share the fact that I was a pastor with a few select members of my A.A. groups, but no one knew in my congregation. Through a number of unique circumstances, including dropping my sobriety coin, I am gradually telling people in my present congregation of my alcoholism and recovery. It has been quite liberating for me. The response has been one of acceptance and support.

By God's grace, the support of FRLC, A.A., prayer, and reading I am now approaching my fourth anniversary of sobriety. My family is proud of me, and my colleagues respect me. I don't use the words "sophisticated drunk" anymore at A.A. meetings. Others started using it and I realized that there was nothing sophisticated about alcoholic drinking. I don't know if it is sophisticated or not, but carrying the message of A.A. and FRLC to others

Our Stories of Experience, Strength, & Hope

is exciting and liberating. I still encounter problems in my ministry and life, but I now meet them with new found courage and hope.

by the Fellowship of Recovering Lutheran Clergy

"It was with a lot of trepidation and uncertainty that I entered the treatment center in Arizona, and I will never forget the words of the treatment center medical director upon my admission: "I am a recovering alcoholic and a workaholic. Quite frankly, it has been much more of a struggle to deal with my workaholism."

"So, I knew I was facing one of the greatest challenges of my life."

--*Rev. Elwood R.*

Who says you shouldn't work hard? Isn't that how you "get ahead"? Isn't that how you get things done? Isn't that the message that we hear over and over again in our culture? We do it "the old fashioned way"- we work hard; and if we work long enough and hard enough, there will be a good reward in the end. And especially if you are "working for the Lord," who can argue with that?

Our Stories of Experience, Strength, & Hope

That was the message that I learned from my dad early in life. It was never spoken but oh how it was practiced day after day. Dad always seemed to be up early, making sure that the sawdust-burning furnace in the basement was functioning property. A quick breakfast and then he'd be off to work.

Work was only three blocks away, so he would often walk. And he must have been the fastest walker in town. Once in awhile when I'd walk with him, I'd almost have to trot to keep up with his pace. He'd come home for lunch and supper but usually following supper, he'd go back to work, stating that he had to "work on the books" if business was to proceed properly the next morning.

Dad easily worked a 12- to 14- hour day. And even on weekends, when the business would not be open, it was not uncommon for him to bring some books home in order to make sure that everything would be in order for Monday morning's business. Is it any wonder that I grew up believing that the only way that you get ahead is to work long and hard each day?

I recall years ago, after having become a pastor, attending a workshop and reading a questionnaire which asked, "How many hours a week do you work?" I wrote down: 80. The next question was, "How many hours would you like to work each week?" I indicated: 55. After doing this exercise, it got me to thinking. What would it

57

by the Fellowship of Recovering Lutheran Clergy

feel like to only work 55 hours a week? And would I feel good about myself, would I have put in a "good week's work" if 55 hours was 'air' that I could claim?

This exercise got me to thinking, but sadly it was little more than a fleeting thought. I had answered the questions; I had completed the requirement; but once the workshop was over, I went back to my addictive, workaholic ways.

There is no denying that a pastor is often asked to sit in on and to participate in a lot of committee meetings. And often they are in the evenings, when lay people in the parish are available. Here I was, going back to work after supper, after having spent a full day, studying, completing office work, and making calls on parishioners. I saw my wife and children at meals, but what other quality time was there for them?

I didn't realize that I was living a life-style almost identical to my dad's. I was much more a human doing than a human being. I might have continued to live my life this way with very little insight as to what I was doing to my wife and children, let alone myself, had it not been for a series of changes in my life.

We had experienced a very traumatic time in a congregation in North Dakota and now a new opportunity for call presented itself in Iowa. While still in North Dakota my wife had worked as a nurse in a chemical dependency treatment center. This new opportunity in

Our Stories of Experience, Strength, & Hope

Iowa was to a church that owned a women's halfway house and the congregation was committed in its outreach to A.A. and other 12-Step groups.

When I was extended the call to this congregation, we rejoiced that we would be going to a Christian community where there was sensitivity to the needs of addicted people. Upon arriving in Iowa, we found ourselves talking with people who were part of the A.A. program and who knew what treatment facilities were available in our new city.

At this same time my wife was struggling with the chemical addiction of her second son (my step-son) as well as the consequences of the marriage of her daughter to an alcoholic. The combination of all of this led my wife to go into outpatient co-dependency treatment. Upon completing the treatment, she made some changes in her life that caused me to realize that my life-style left a lot to be desired.

The end result was that I joined a weekly men's group, one that met away from our church and that was headed up by a counselor who was highly recommended by people we knew in the A.A. movement. Through these weekly meetings I soon came to find that I had a "safe" environment, a place where I could share my hurts and struggles in a way that I had never done before. I also found that our counselor was a man of compassion and

by the Fellowship of Recovering Lutheran Clergy

competence, a person who was adept at understanding what my most basic needs were.

Then one day, as we met one-on-one, he challenged me, "Are you willing to give yourself a gift?"

I responded, "What do you mean?"

He continued, "Are you willing to give yourself the gift of going away for a month in order to deal with your addiction to work?"

I was dumbfounded. Who, me? Is it really that serious, that apparent? Do I really need this? And what will people think? And how in the world can I take off a whole month from parish ministry? The questions kept flooding through my mind. I finally pleaded, "I've got to talk with my wife. I've got to think this through." The more I thought about it, the more the idea of gift kept striking me. "Are you willing to give yourself a gift?' I could, as a pastor, talk about the gift of the gospel to each of us. Now, was I willing to accept this gift myself?

In talking with my wife, her understanding and encouragement helped me realize that this was a tremendous gift I could not refuse. Now it was a matter of talking to key people-bishop, associate pastor, congregational president, church council-in order to clear the way and to make preparations for being away from the parish for a month.

Our Stories of Experience, Strength, & Hope

It was with a lot trepidation and uncertainty that I entered the treatment center in Arizona, but I will never forget the words of the treatment center medical director upon my admission: "I am a recovering alcoholic and a workaholic. Quite frankly, it has been much more of a struggle to deal with my workaholicism." So, I knew I was facing one of the greatest challenges of my life.

I met my counselor; I was assigned to my small group; and one of the most meaningful, and I must say painful, 30-day periods of my life began. Working side by side with addicts of all types, I came to see what a privilege it was to be able to entrust myself to the care of all the counselors who were a part of this center. And I came to see, as it oftentimes has been said, "Treatment is a time of discovery; what follows afterward (and for the rest of one's life) is recovery."

It certainly was a time of discovery, to realize how working long hours had become a god for me, to be confronted with and to identify my perfectionism. It was a journey through each of the Steps, climaxing in the fourth and then fifth Step, but continuing all the way through to Step 12. I benefited from the holistic approach of the center, taking full advantage of the variety of physical activities such as weight-lifting, exercise equipment, swimming, horseback riding, and hiking. And the third week was family week when my wife and youngest

by the Fellowship of Recovering Lutheran Clergy

daughter were able to attend and together we could look at my issues.

This whole experience enabled me to look at myself through new glasses, to see my daily need for God's grace, and to recognize I am so similar to so many other people in this world. As the entire course of treatment drew to a close, with the help of my counselor, we put together a three-part treatment plan that was to be so beneficial in the weeks and months that lay ahead: 1) to find a sponsor and to meet with that person on a regular basis, 2) to regularly attend my weekly men's group, and 3) to go to at least one 12-Step meeting weekly. The plan was in place, and I was ready to re-enter the real world.

I came back to my community and congregation wondering just what it would be like. People in the congregation greeted me with words such as "nice to have you back," but there was little more that I sensed they were able to say. In a Bible study, in an adult forum, or in some small group session, most people were noticeably uncomfortable dealing with the idea of workaholism.

Occasionally someone would ask, "Please help me. I don't really understand why you were gone for a month. What is workaholism, especially in the life of a pastor?" The implication often was: 'We have called you to be our pastor and we know that that often requires many hours of counseling and other challenges that will stretch your

Our Stories of Experience, Strength, & Hope

endurance. Why is it that you label yourself a workaholic when other pastors seem to handle the responsibilities of parish life fairly well?"

I felt like saying that a lot of pastors I know are not handling it that well, but rather I simply tried when appropriate to talk about what an addiction is and how any good thing can become a god. Some people seemed to understand, many did not, and I accepted the fact they simply hadn't walked in my shoes.

I basically expressed appreciation to congregational members for the opportunity to be gone for a month to work on issues in my personal life and that all of us were part of a church (local and national) that saw the need for pastors to get help and that our church supported this spiritually and financially.

My biggest disappointment and feeling of abandonment came from fellow pastors in neighboring Lutheran congregations. We had a weekly pastoral Scripture text study group that I regularly attended. On my return I was greeted with words such as, "So, you're back. How's your life? Any different?" Or, "Did you get everything all straightened out?" It was said with little compassion, almost bordering on sarcasm. It hurt; but inwardly I thanked God for the great gift that I had received, even if my fellow pastors couldn't appreciate it.

by the Fellowship of Recovering Lutheran Clergy

My wife understood and supported me and a number of people in the 12-Step movement stood by me.

The treatment plan, outlined for me in the final days that I was away, proved to be key in the initial weeks and months of recovery. I found a sponsor, a person who weekly participated in his own 12-Step meetings; and he and I met on a regular basis. Initially it was every week, then once every two weeks. We continued to meet this way for nine years (until I subsequently retired from parish ministry and moved out of state).

As for the men's group, I was welcomed back to it with open arms and I found it so renewing and enriching to be able to openly to talk with people who understood what I was saying. Needless to say, the counselor who had been so instrumental in getting me to go into treatment was the most supportive and understanding of all. I continued with the weekly meetings of this group for eight years.

I also found a meaningful 12-Step meeting that I faithfully attended for five years. I can't say enough for following such a treatment plan. My walk in recovery would not have been possible without it. Incidentally, I reduced my weekly work hours to 55. I took time first thing each morning physically to work out. As a result I usually would get to the office around 9:30 a.m.., feeling refreshed and much more relaxed for the challenges of the day.

Our Stories of Experience, Strength, & Hope

Since my retirement from parish ministry in the fall of 1999, the stresses and responsibilities in my life are greatly reduced. My wife and I are active in our local congregation, and we have been able to serve as co-facilitators of a congregation-based Christian ministry to people struggling with addictions. We also have started a weekly co-dependency group since such a group did not exist in our area. Both of our pastors are very supportive of the 12-Step movement, and this makes it a joy to live and worship in such a Christian environment.

I know that I will always need the encouragement of an understanding wife, of fellow recovering people in the 12-Step movement, of access to good reading material, of being able to attend 12-Step meetings, and, of course, of being in relationship with a God who meets me daily as a sinner saved by grace. I am so thankful for all of God's gifts so abundantly provided in my life.

by the Fellowship of Recovering Lutheran Clergy

"I had always suspected that there was something wrong with me, only I didn't know what it was."

I was also terrified that if the church knew who I really was they would want no part of me.
--Rev. Melanie M.

My name is Melanie and I'm an alcoholic and addict. I am also a woman and a pastor. In reality I qualified for the first two labels by the time I was 15. Growing up in the '60s and '70s, it seemed like the easiest and best way to deal with the pain in my life.

At age 17, during my first quarter of college, I "hit bottom." I prayed to God for help—and met a new man. This was the beginning of what I now call my "functioning-in-life-practicing-alcoholic" stage. Only I didn't have the words for it until much later.

In my second year of seminary, with much fear and trepidation, I signed up for a class in alcoholism. God had set me up for it in a way. I had spent the summer working at a resort where the 40-something chronic alcoholic son came home to manage the restaurant because he couldn't hold down a real job. As the summer progressed, I

Our Stories of Experience, Strength, & Hope

realized that I had no idea how to help him; and, in fact, I was quite anxious about the whole subject. So come fall quarter, I registered for a life-changing experience.

By the grace of God the class was taught by a Lutheran pastor who was also alcoholic. He had been sober for 10 years at the time, which seemed like forever to me. Knowing that he was "one of them" and was still a pastor gave me the courage to look at myself honestly. I had always suspected that there was something wrong with me, only I didn't know what it was. I was also terrified that if the church knew who I really was, they would want no part of me. By looking at him I was able to grasp on to a slender thread that there might be hope for me too.

The class was assigned to attend open Alcoholic Anonymous meetings, read the "Big Book" of Alcoholics Anonymous and, in class, role play what goes on in A.A. meetings. We did some other reading as well, and it seemed that each week I read or heard about something I had done.

Time and time again I asked my instructor, "What does this mean if I've done such and such?" I entered a phase of intense questioning like I'd never gone through in my life before. Was I or wasn't I? If I was, was I sick enough to get well? Or was I too sick for recovery to happen and doomed to a life of destruction and eventual death?

by the Fellowship of Recovering Lutheran Clergy

I went out and got drunk, depressed by the whole struggle. I stayed sober for a while, then drank again, afraid of what my friends and seminary classmates would think if I told the truth. I called for help and I pushed the offered hand away. I babysat a friend's child on New Year's Eve in an effort to stay sober and finally, on the Eve of Epiphany 1980, got drunk for the last time, an unglamorous day locked in my bedroom with a bottle.

My overwhelming sense of shame and fear of rejection by the church stayed with me a long time. I struggled through several encounters with my synod's leadership preparation committee, practically daring them to kick me out. Fortunately for me, some enlightened souls in that group were exceedingly patient and caring. They reassured me that having a problem was "not the end of the world" and that they were much more worried about those who had a problem but didn't realize it.

I graduated from seminary, and kept both my disease and my recovery a secret for the most part through my first call. "After all," I thought, "it's hard enough for women to get a call in the church without giving them another excuse to reject me."

During my second call, I was a little braver, though not by much. I didn't discuss my alcoholism at interview time, but I did reveal it in my first sermon. I clearly saw those who were put off by my revelation, and was blind to those who affirmed my openness. (My husband reminded me that the congregation applauded that sermon, a fact I did not remember at all.) I backtracked into hiding for several more years.

Finally, as I was nearing my tenth anniversary of sobriety, it dawned on me that it was time to open up. By this time, I'd been a pastor for eight years, felt good about my ministry in a congregation, preached at the constituting convention of our synod, and had been elected to synod council. I knew the bishop and staff well and was on good terms with them. I figured if I wasn't secure enough to be public about it now, I never would be.

I talked to my bishop. I talked to my secretary. I talked to the congregation. I talked to the fellow who helps pastors in trouble. I felt like a great burden had lifted. I finally felt free—because others knew who I was and they loved me anyway. It was an experience of the grace of God given through the church in a whole new way.

Then the phone rang. Would I help a seminarian who was struggling with his own drinking? Thinking back to my own days as a seminarian and how I never would have made it without my teacher friend who shared his experience, strength, and hope with me, I quickly said yes. I also thought, "There's got to be a better way—some sort of network or system where clergy who are just becoming aware of their disease can make contact with those who

by the Fellowship of Recovering Lutheran Clergy

have gone before them. There has got to be some way that those of us who've been around awhile can touch base with each other for mutual sharing and support."

I began exploring options for doing that and eventually sent a letter to the dozen or so Lutheran clergy in recovery whom I knew, asking for their ideas and input. I started a grass roots newsletter called Lutheran Clergy in Recovery Network (LCRN) to share stories and information about clergy in recovery. I sent it to everyone I knew, a few treatment centers, and others I heard of who might be interested.

Imagine my surprise when a few months later I received a phone call from a Lutheran Church, a Missouri Synod pastor working on the same idea! It was as if God had taken this task and divided it up: one male, one female; one east coast, one west coast; one ELCA, one LCMS; one working on the organizational/funding side, one working on the networking connections side.

My new partner, after attending a retreat sponsored by RACA (the Recovering Alcoholic Clergy Association of the Episcopal Church) initiated the Fellowship of Recovering Lutheran Clergy. This fellowship officially began meeting in April 1991 at the Chicago Holiday Inn. Since then the fellowship has grown to more than 200 members.

Our Stories of Experience, Strength, & Hope

I share my story for a couple of reasons. First of all, I hope to give encouragement to those who may still be struggling with this disease. Secondly, I hope those of you who are not addicted will learn more about the disease, have compassion, and reach out with an open hand to colleagues who are suffering.

by the Fellowship of Recovering Lutheran Clergy

"My creativity led me to believe that I could do anything and deal with any situation."

"It was a classic example of grandiosity."
--Rev. Al D.

My name is Al and I'm a recovering Adult Child from an Alcoholic Family (ACOA). Alcohol and prescription drug addiction of close family members had a powerful and detrimental effect on my life until I was led into recovery in March of 1983. Since then I have had an ongoing and healing relationship with the 12 Steps of Al Anon and CODA. The word gratitude can hardly express how I feel about my life today. My Higher Power has blessed me richly and continues to do so as I work my program.

I believe that my birth father had a serious drinking problem when I was born, and he may have well been addicted to alcohol by that time. What I can remember of him (he and my mother were divorced when I was seven) shows all the earmarks of alcoholism. He drank heavily; he was physically abusive to my mother and me; he had a series of affairs; he stole from his employer; and, after the divorce, he abandoned my mother, my sister and me financially. The last time I saw him was on my 11th

Our Stories of Experience, Strength, & Hope

birthday when he brought me a bicycle. He died in 1990, and I learned about his death about nine months later.

Never having had a father during those early formative years made it extremely difficult later when I married and began to have a family of my own. Somehow I muddled through as a husband and parent, but I know that there were many things that I missed. This caused me great regret early in my recovery because of all the lost opportunities; but I have learned that I can be a good, caring husband and father now and I do my best to be that.

My mother came from an alcoholic family. My maternal grandparents were immigrants from Denmark and Sweden. Her father and brother were addicted to alcohol; and one of her sisters was addicted to alcohol, nicotine and prescription drugs. My grandmother was very codependent to the situation but she was a very kind and loving woman. My mother was in ongoing conflict with her father and this caused her to become very controlling. I'm sure that when she married my father, between his alcoholism and her codependence, there were probably many power struggles.

I grew up in a small town in the Pacific Northwest and attended grade school there until the middle of grade six. At that point my mother remarried and we moved to a small city where I continued my schooling until I graduated from high school.

by the Fellowship of Recovering Lutheran Clergy

My stepfather adopted me several years after he and my mother married and I took his name. He was a kind man and we became close. He loved to fish and hunt and taught me to do both, although today I do neither.

I lived what I thought was a normal life throughout my school years. I had good friends, I was active in school activities, and I was an excellent student. What I didn't know then and didn't recognize until many years later was that I had become the hero child in my family, and this is what drove my desire to belong and achieve.

When I went to college, I was looking for a wife; and I found a beautiful young woman in my second year who agreed to marry me. We were married in 1958 and are still married. What I didn't realize was that my ACOA background would be the basis for continued conflict throughout the marriage because of my codependency. I have worked hard to address this and believe that God has given me the ability and the desire to change how I relate to my wife. I was very controlling, which should be no surprise to anyone given my background. I'm sure this caused a lot of heartache for my wife over the years.

We have four children, two girls and two boys and, currently, seven grandchildren. Each of them is a real joy to me and I'm really proud of who they are.

I attended seminary and graduated in 1963. My pattern of accepting and working in a call situation was a typical

Our Stories of Experience, Strength, & Hope

geographical escape process although I didn't recognize it at the time. I served two parishes, directed a Bible Camp and worked on the national level of the denominational youth staff within a 14-year period. My creativity led me to believe that I could do anything and deal with any situation. It was a classic example of grandiosity.

My recovery began in 1977 when I was fired from the position on our denominational youth staff. I had taken this position not realizing that the person in charge was an extremely conflicted individual who projected his pain onto various staff members. Over a three-year period the pressure of how I was being treated built until I finally exploded at him and said some very damaging things. I was then informed that I was no longer capable of doing the job. I took several short-term positions to keep money coming in and a year later, in desperation, accepted a call to an inner city congregation. I've since learned that when a person does something in desperation he usually pays and pays and pays. I did.

A year and a half later I was fired again, and I believe I was led by God to begin working in an outpatient drug and alcohol treatment center. While there I began to learn about alcoholic families and realized that this was my background.

Little by little the message of this program and my continuing exposure to the 12 Steps began to sink in.

by the Fellowship of Recovering Lutheran Clergy

I decided to become an addiction counselor and began training at the University of Houston. One night at one of the lectures I heard a list read that astonished me because every item on it was true of me in one way or another as an ACOA. I broke down and began to cry and cried throughout the lecture. It was at that point that I realized that I needed counseling to begin dealing with all the chaos that was present in my life. That's when my recovery formally began.

About a year later, in 1984, my wife's company transferred her to the East Coast where we have lived since. I began a career as an addiction counselor with a local interdenominational mental health agency and after three years with them moved into private practice. I retired from that practice in December 1999.

As part of my recovery I was instrumental in starting an Al Anon group for adult children and still attend those meetings. I also attend CODA because I realize that my codependency continues to be cunning, baffling and powerful. I have experienced a number of relapses in my recovery; and they have taught me that progress, not perfection, is what it's all about. In fact, I am grateful for my relapses because they have given me the opportunity to rethink what recovery is about and how important it is to work this program on a daily basis. I believe that this program is life-long and that as long as I'm alive, I'll benefit from it.

One important thing, probably the most important, is that this program has introduced me to a spiritual way of living. I received an excellent theological education over the years, beginning with Sunday school and continuing through college, seminary and graduate work. But I learned nothing in any of those situations about my spiritual self. The 12 Steps have shown me how rich a life in the spirit can be and I rejoice in that daily. I have a spiritual director who has become both a treasured guide and good friend. I continue to ask for openness so that I may grow in seeking God's will for my life. How blessed I am.

by the Fellowship of Recovering Lutheran Clergy

"I decided to go into treatment. To this day I remember it as the most terrifying, most humiliating, best day of my life."

"It was the day my life changed forever."
--Rev. Ed T.

I grew up in a Catholic, military family. We moved 32 times in 20 years. During that time we attended mass faithfully. Other than praying at meal times, religion was not a regular part of our home life.

My father grew up during the Depression. He worked for everything he had from his earliest childhood on. He also came from a broken home. My father didn't have a drinking problem, but he grew up in a dysfunctional home and therefore manifested the disease in his life in other ways. My mother was a classic co-dependent and enabler. Our home was chaotic and unpredictable. We never knew what was going to happen from one minute to the next in our home. Besides the chaos, we were expected to be perfect. Unfortunately the definition of perfection was never very clear; and no matter how hard we tried, the rules were sure to change from one day to the next. The goalposts were always being moved beyond my reach. I

Our Stories of Experience, Strength, & Hope

was never quite good enough. I could never seem to get it right.

When my father retired we moved into civilian life. Dad was busy with his career and mom had eight kids to feed, so I could pretty much come and go as I pleased. I fell in with the neighborhood boys and began experimenting with cigarettes, booze, and marijuana. I will never forget how it felt the first time I drank. When that warm, wonderful feeling came over me I forgot who I was. For the first time in my life I felt good on the inside. I became funny and charming and totally unself-conscious.

We stole alcohol from our parents as often as we could. We always joked that dad never became an alcoholic because so many of us kids stole his booze from him, he was never really drinking anything but colored water.

I attended every party I could find through high school, even hosting many. I had a fake ID and could buy kegs of beer when I was 15. I tried many other things too, like LSD, speed, cocaine, mushrooms, lsd, and heroin. If it was available, I would give it a go. I sold drugs as well.

After high school I moved to Maui, Hawaii, to live the good life for awhile.

I worked in the food and hotel industry and would be out every night closing down the bars, looking for some excitement. During that time I got my real estate license

by the Fellowship of Recovering Lutheran Clergy

and worked for a realtor as a property manager. Still the partier, I could never quite figure out why I couldn't seem to get my life together. I really didn't think my behavior was that unusual. Didn't everybody go out after work?

I finally decided my problem was where I was living. I thought if I could get a fresh start somewhere else, I could make things work. I traded my car for a bag of Maui Wowie, skipped out on my landlord and boss and headed to San Diego.

My brother lived in San Diego with his girlfriend. I surprised them by showing up on their steps with all my belongings. I lived on their couch for about two months. My brother and I smoked up the weed or traded it for cocaine. When the dope ran out, so did my brother's girlfriend's patience. I had to find a job, or move on.

I decided to hitchhike back to Washington, where my family lived; but I caught a ride to Phoenix instead, because an old high school buddy was living there. He let me move in; and with my great restaurant experience, I landed a job in a French restaurant in Scottsdale, making several hundred dollars a night in tips.

For three years I stayed in Phoenix, drinking, smoking, and sniffing all my tips away every night. I finally decided what I needed was a fresh start somewhere else. I moved back to Bellingham, Washington, and went to work as a waiter again, this time with lousy tips. Nothing much

Our Stories of Experience, Strength, & Hope

changed in my life, except for the fact that now I was into shooting cocaine into my veins on occasion. I knew there was something wrong with me; but I had this firm belief that if I could just pull my act together, I could get things under control. I just needed to find the right woman, start exercising, keep my apartment clean, start a savings account, and get the right job. I was baffled as to why I couldn't get those things to happen in my life. I can't count the number of times I've tried to straighten up--with sincere desire.

I was eventually offered a job as a restaurant manager, which was great because the restaurant had a well-stocked bar. When the inventory kept coming up short, they caught on to me and let me go.

I got on with another restaurant, and they ended up firing me, too. I had a bad attitude, I was hung over too often, then finally I called the boss's wife a four-letter word one morning. I finally decided what I needed was a fresh start somewhere else.

I moved to Lake Tahoe where an old high school buddy was tending bar. When I arrived, we took my $700.00 life savings and bought a quarter ounce of cocaine, hoping to sell it for a good profit. Business was slow that night, so we ended up free-basing (smoking) just about all of it.

by the Fellowship of Recovering Lutheran Clergy

I will never forget how I felt the next morning. I came to in my friend's house, on the floor, where there was a strong smell of stale beer and dog poop. My throat was so swollen from smoking the cocaine I could hardly breathe. The realization of my situation hit me hard. Here I was, starting my life over again. I was completely broke. I was living in a strange new place. I was looking for work—again! I couldn't take it anymore.

I called home; and when I heard my mother's voice, I began to cry. She had been trying to get me into treatment for some time. My brother had taken me to A.A. meetings, but I had concluded it was a place for people who didn't know God. I knew God, and I knew God would save my life without making me have to go to a pitiful place like Alcoholics Anonymous. I wanted a miracle, not A.A.

Mom suggested I go into treatment, and I still couldn't see the need. I was having life problems, not drug problems. I didn't use that much; and if I could just get my life together, I probably would hardly use at all, I reasoned--truly believing myself.

The next day mom called back with a phone number of a treatment center near me. She said, "If you want help, that's where you will get it. That's all I can do for you." It was a pretty gutsy move for a mom talking to a desperate son. It was the best thing she ever did for me in my life.

Our Stories of Experience, Strength, & Hope

I decided to go into treatment. To this day I remember it as the most terrifying, most humiliating day of my life. It was the day my life changed forever.

I spent three days in detox where I read the entire A.A. Big Book. It was amazing to learn about alcoholism and addiction. It was so clear to me then that this was exactly what I was dealing with. It explained everything, my whole life.

I attended A.A. meetings and have been now for the last 15 years. Those first few years were a struggle, to say the least. I did have a few slips, but they were reminders of what I never want to go back to.

In my first year of sobriety I decided to go back to school. I had to enroll in a community college, as my high school grades were so poor. I completed my two year degree with honors and transferred to a state university. I completed my degree in journalism and became a writer for a local newspaper.

In my last year of college a friend and I were traveling through the Cascade Mountains on a spiritual quest when we stumbled into Holden Village, an ex-mining camp that operates now as a Lutheran retreat center. I knew nothing about Lutherans, and I was very surprised to find on the weekend we were there they were hosting a 12-Step workshop for people in recovery.

by the Fellowship of Recovering Lutheran Clergy

I had given up on the church in my early sobriety. I had decided that if Jesus were alive today, he would not be in the church, but rather would be in 12 Step meetings where the broken are greeted and welcomed without condition and loved back into life. I didn't see the church doing that very much. But Holden Village was a homecoming for me. The liturgy of worship resonated with my Catholic past and the theology of the cross made perfect sense to me.

I joined a local Lutheran church and got involved with Holden Village, spending a summer there as a volunteer. During that summer I met my wife, Karen, from Minnesota. After we married, a year later we returned to Holden. I had been struggling with my career choice; and during a morning run at Holden, I felt a strong sense that I needed to be closer to God. I decided the way to do that was to go to a school and to study the Bible and theology. I told Karen I wanted to go to seminary. She thought I said I wanted to be a pastor, but that was the last thing on my mind. I just wanted to study God.

I applied to the seminary and was accepted. During my time there, God tricked me into becoming a pastor. In 1995 I graduated and took a call in rural Nebraska where I spent four good years.

Currently I am living in suburban Minneapolis where I have the joy and challenge of developing a new congregation as a mission developer. So far things are going amazingly well. The church is organized and growing. We have a 12 Step group that meets every Monday night. I have three beautiful children (a fourth on the way), I exercise, I maintain a savings account, I sleep well, I eat well, I make my bed in the morning. I know peace and joy. I know serenity.

During all those years of pain and misery I prayed countless prayers that God would rescue me. All I wanted was for the madness in my life to stop. What I got was far more than that. God answers prayers--not always in the way we expect, not with the speed we would like, but God always gives us more than we deserve.

It was during seminary I first heard about the Fellowship of Recovering Lutheran Clergy. I attended their first retreat in Chicago and what a joy it was to discover there were other clergy who have lived through some of the same things I have. Though I was not ordained when I was addicted, I can only imagine how awful it must be for a member of the clergy living in the nightmare of addiction while serving as a pastor. If that is you, I hope you will reach out for help. You are not alone.

by the Fellowship of Recovering Lutheran Clergy

"It continues to amuse me how humans "normalize" the behaviors of the family in which we grow up."

". . . my self-esteem was in the cellar, which put me at the mercy of older, seemingly more confident, boys. If I thought a behavior would raise my status, I would do it-- regardless of risk!"

--Pastor Dick W.

Dear Suffering Servant:

Hi! My name is Dick, and I'm an alcoholic.

I was born into the strictest, noncharismatic, fundamentalist sect in the southern U.S. My mother taught the Bible for 60 years. If there had been any organization above the congregational level (and there was not), everybody agreed that my maternal grandfather would have been the bishop of Oklahoma. He was a wonderful gentleman, and I loved him dearly.

My paternal grandfather (pgf), on the other hand, couldn't have been more opposite. My earliest memory of him is when I was probably five years old. He pinched up some skin on my waist and kept pinching harder until I ran screaming from the room. I think he didn't care for children and he found a way to have them keep their distance. It worked! His personal habits were none too attractive, either. The code word in our family, if a male had left his pants unzipped, was my pgf's name.

My dad and his two brothers chipped in and bought a 160-acre piece of land, covered by scrub-oak except for a small lake and a small log cabin. The cabin was the main attraction, so my pgf could have a place to live. This kept him from being a skid-row bum. They imported his brother, Walter, to keep house for him. Some thought it was the first steady job Walter had ever had.

It continues to amuse me how humans "normalize" the behaviors of the family in which we grow up. Since my parents' church considered the first drink a sin, it was almost impossible for me to imagine anyone of my immediate family (including my pgf) drinking. I remember naively wondering who hauled in those whisky and beer bottles and put them in that 55-gallon oil drum out behind my pgf's log cabin.

My father claimed to have never had a drink in his life and I have no reason to doubt this. However, I am convinced that he was mentally ill and he was addicted to prescription drugs. I am not sure at what age he began to physically abuse me, but I can remember his holding me off the floor with one hand while he beat me with his belt with the other hand. Perhaps I was three or four.

by the Fellowship of Recovering Lutheran Clergy

Like most addicts, my father was unpredictable and volatile. Because he didn't smell of alcohol, I believed that the blurry eyes were from hay-fever and that left no real clues. I, of course, tried to "normalize" his behavior and I came to believe that all boys were punished in the same way - they too were just good at not "talking out of school" about family matters.

I could be mistaken, but I believe with all of my heart that my father never said anything nice about me to me. My mother told me that he bragged about me to their friends, but he never told me. To my knowledge, he never laid a hand on my sister. His nicknames for us tell the story: hers was "Sweetie Pie," mine was "Hammerhead." He said he was making me into "a real man."

My father was "into leather," and graduated from his belt to a horse quirt. This is a two-foot long stiff riding-crop with braided raw-hide covering. He once beat me with the quirt until I had bloody welts all over my body. I was unable to deal with this --or even acknowledge it-- until I was in my mid-thirties. Needless to say, my self-esteem was in the cellar, which put me at the mercy of older, seemingly more confident, boys. If I thought a behavior would raise my status, I would do it-- regardless of risk!

When I was 12, I went with my rich cousin to his parents' lake home. As soon as the adults were out of sight

Our Stories of Experience, Strength, & Hope

on the cabin-cruiser, my cousin, who was two years older, said he and his friend were going to have a drink and did I want one? I believe that I did not have enough self-esteem to say "No!"

So he and the other older boy (the preacher's kid) mixed us drinks with limeade and rum (it's sort of a daiquiri). It was hot, and I drank mine rather quickly. Then, I had another. I had never seen a drink mixed, so I made it way too strong, but I didn't mind. But I did begin to feel funny. I remember that my cowboy boots seemed to grow a couple of inches, and my chest-size expanded. The hair stood up on the back of my neck, and I WAS A REAL MAN.

I felt a bit woozy and I thought a bit of air would help. My cousin had a hydro-plane, and I took it out on this huge reservoir. As soon as I got it up to top speed, I began to feel tired, so I put my head down for just a moment. When I looked up, I was almost on the rocks on the far side of the lake. I got it stopped, and turned around, and I decided to return a bit slower. But, whereas I had been just hitting the tops of the waves on the way over, on the return trip the boat took more of an up-and-down motion. By the time I docked, I was really sick. I got a couple of handfuls of a willow bush on the shore, and I vomited, and I puked, and I up-chucked, and I flashed hash, and I got the "dry-heaves." I remember that there was something hanging

by the Fellowship of Recovering Lutheran Clergy

from the back of my throat that wouldn't detach, so I had to pinch it off with my fingers.

Now, I was considered to be the smartest kid in our church community. I had just had my first experience with the chemical. The first time I drank, I got drunk! I got so drunk that I almost killed myself! I got so sick that I wished I had died. Now there were a lot of possible lessons to be had from this chemical encounter. But what I took away from there that day was "Indelibly etched on the psyche was the irresistible impulse to repeat the experience of intoxication." I knew I was going to do that again--as often as I could.

In that same summer, the first summer out of the sixth grade, I was introduced to another way to take away my pain. A friend and I were walking when we encountered a boy we knew who said "Hey, you want to get laid?" Again, I believe that I had no ego-strength to draw on to say, "Are you kidding, I'm only 12, I don't even shave!" I will forever be grateful to that girl--she told me everything that I wanted to hear. She told me that I was the best. I felt LIKE A REAL MAN! From that day on, I tried to do both of those pain-alleviating behaviors, as often as I could-- alcohol and sex.

And, for the next 20 years, I drank out of control and was involved romantically, almost without ceasing. I was married and divorced several times. The sex/romance would get me into the marriage, and I would drink my way out. The only occupation I was qualified for was "Student." And I stretched it out as long as I could. My record is appalling, resembling a roller-coaster. One semester I made 14 hours of "F;" the next I made the Dean's List. Then, my success would convince me that I could drink like a gentleman, so I would go right back to failure.

At one point, my parents disowned me. They wouldn't permit me to talk to them or visit their home. They saw their lawyer and wrote me out of their wills. I went to work for a year in the oil field. It was actually good for me. Then back to school.

When I wasn't paying close attention, I wound up doing a short stint in the army. Again, when I wasn't being careful, I graduated. There I was, with no skills and a lousy GPA. There was only one thing to do. I went to law school.

But, I made a geographical cure - I went to Minnesota - 900 miles away! I thought, "I can make a fresh start. I haven't thrown up on anybody here, yet." But, it was the same old story. My drinking got worse and worse. My current wife left and I dropped out of school, again. Discovering that she had a long history of not being sexually faithful in our marriage provided me with all the motivation I needed to drink myself into oblivion.

by the Fellowship of Recovering Lutheran Clergy

But, a funny thing happened. I got my grades, and I had not flunked out. So, back to academia I went. It seems that I had learned how to write the exams. I didn't make any "A"s, but I didn't flunk out as a third of our class did. And, of course, I had a new romance. One night when I was so drunk that I was ejected from the party by my heavy-drinking friends, she said to me "My father was an alcoholic, and, my God, I've gone out and found me one." She threatened to leave me unless I stopped drinking. I thought I would just stop until I was sure she wouldn't leave. I had my only experience with "D.T."s. It scared me straight. I was only 25 years old.

My mother came to visit me and said, "Honey, we are all so proud that you have stopped drinking--we've know for a long time what a terrible drinking problem you have." That was news to me! "But," she said, "You are so nervous." She reached into her purse and came up with a large jar of pills. "Just take one of these in the morning, one at noon and two at bedtime--and my doctor says they aren't habit-forming--they will just take the highs and the lows off." Well, she was right--except for the non-addicting part. "You say that you are having difficulty sleeping?" She went back into her purse for another container and admitted that "These might be habit forming, so don't take them every day." I didn't. I didn't take them on Thursdays!

Our Stories of Experience, Strength, & Hope

I had quit drinking before, many times. I was convinced that I could quit for any length of time--as long as I knew that, at the end, I could begin again. This time, I didn't have a drink for four and a half years. I was introduced, years later, as an A.A. speaker, by a man who said "Dick W. is the only person I have ever known who stayed dry four and a half years *through prayer and medication.*"

Through a funny set of circumstances, I was trying to help a friend get sober, when I was told to join Alcoholics Anonymous. When my friend got out of treatment, we both joined. I was a snotty young lawyer who thought I could whip this thing by myself. I would just go to these meetings long enough to figure out what it was they did to stay sober, then I wouldn't have to go to these stupid meetings any more. I didn't really work the "steps"-- I just recited them. Then, I had a life crisis and no real program to hold onto. So, I wound up having some sort of a breakdown. The interesting thing, from a masculine psychology standpoint, is that I never stopped performing. I tried my most important case while melting down. And I won even the points I thought we would lose. I only mention this to dispel the myth that if your job doesn't suffer, you must be all right. I was not all right. My psychiatric diagnosis was "psychotic episode." They treated me for alcoholism, and it changed my life.

by the Fellowship of Recovering Lutheran Clergy

    I wound up leaving the law practice the same year my biography appeared in "Who's Who in American Law" 2nd ed. I completed the course work and worked as a counselor in chemical dependency for 16 years. At age 52 I entered seminary. I was ordained at age 56. I was called to a mission congregation that is 240 miles from the nearest church of the same denomination. We have just worshiped the third Sunday in our new church building. I have been married for the last time for 16 years to a European artist. We enjoy a full and exciting life. But, most important, the sine qua non for all the rest is that this St. Patrick's Day my A.A. group presented me with a 31 year medallion. Praise God!

The Twelve Steps of Alcoholics Anonymous*

1. We admitted we were powerless over alcohol that our lives had become unmanageable.
2. Came to believe that a Power greater than ourselves could restore us to sanity.
3. Made a decision to turn our will and our lives over to the care of God *as we understood Him.*
4. Made a searching and fearless moral inventory of ourselves.
5. Admitted to God, to ourselves and to another human being the exact nature of our wrongs.
6. Were entirely ready to have God remove all these defects of character.
7. Humbly asked Him to remove our shortcomings.
8. Made a list of all persons we had harmed, and became willing to make amends to them all.
9. Made direct amends to such people wherever possible, except when to do so would injure them or others.
10. Continued to take personal inventory and when we were wrong promptly admitted it.
11. Sought through prayer and meditation to improve our conscious contact with God, *as we understood Him,* praying only for knowledge of His will for us and the power to carry that out.

by the Fellowship of Recovering Lutheran Clergy

12. Having had a spiritual awakening as the result of these Steps, we tried to carry this message to alcoholics, and to practice these principles in all our affairs.

Step One As Adapted for the FRLC*

1. We admitted we were powerless over alcohol (work, drugs, co-dependency, sin…)— that our lives had become unmanageable.

---

* The Twelve Steps and Twelve Traditions of Alcoholics Anonymous have been reprinted and adapted with the permission of Alcoholics Anonymous World Services, Inc. ("A.A.W.S."). Permission to reprint and adapt the Twelve Steps and Twelve Traditions does not mean that Alcoholics Anonymous is affiliated with this program. A.A. is a program of recovery from alcoholism <u>only</u> – use of A.A.'s Steps and Traditions or an adapted version of its Steps and Traditions in connection with programs and activities which are patterned after A.A., but which address other problems, or use in any other non-A.A. context, does not imply otherwise. Although Alcoholics Anonymous is a spiritual program, A.A. is not a religious program, and use of A.A. material in the present connection does not imply A.A.'s affiliation with or

The Twelve Traditions of Alcoholics Anonymous

1. Our common welfare should come first; personal recovery depends upon A.A. unity.
2. For our group purpose there is but one ultimate authority — a loving God as He may express Himself in our group conscience. Our leaders are but trusted servants; they do not govern.
3. The only requirement for A.A. membership is a desire to stop drinking.
4. Each group should be autonomous except in matters affecting other groups or A.A. as a whole.
5. Each group has but one primary purpose — to carry its message to the alcoholic who still suffers.
6. An A.A. group ought never endorse, finance, or lend the A.A. name to any related facility or outside enterprise, lest problems of money, property, and prestige divert us from our primary spiritual purpose.
7. Every A.A. group ought to be fully self-supporting, declining outside contributions.

---

endorsement of, any sect, denomination, or specific religious belief.

8. Alcoholics Anonymous should remain forever non-professional, but our service centers may employ special workers.
9. A.A., as such, ought never be organized; but we may create service boards or committees directly responsible to those they serve.
10. Alcoholics Anonymous has no opinion on outside issues; hence the A.A. name ought never be drawn into public controversy.
11. Our public relations policy is based on attraction rather than promotion; we need always maintain personal anonymity at the level of press, radio, and films.
12. Anonymity is the spiritual foundation of all our traditions, ever reminding us to place principles before personalities.

Only you can decide whether you want to give A.A. a try —whether you think it can help you.*

The following twelve questions have been excerpted from material appearing in the pamphlet, "Is A.A. for You?", and has been reprinted with permission of Alcoholics Anonymous World Services, Inc. ("A.A.W.S."). Permission to reprint this material does not mean that A.A.W.S. has reviewed and/or endorsed this publication. A. A. is a program of recovery from alcoholism only – use of A.A. material in anly non-A.A. context does not imply otherwise.

We who are in A.A. came because we finally gave up trying to control our drinking. We still hated to admit that we could never drink safely. Then we heard from other A.A. members that we were sick. (We thought so for years!) We found out that many people suffered from the same feelings of guilt and loneliness and hopelessness that we did. We found out that we had these feelings because we had the disease of alcoholism.

We decided to try and face up to what alcohol had done to us. Here are some of the questions we tried to answer *honestly*. If we answered YES to four or more questions, we were in deep trouble with our drinking. See

Our Stories of Experience, Strength, & Hope

how you do. Remember, there is no disgrace in facing up to the fact that you have a problem.

Answer YES or NO to the following questions.

Top of Form

1 - **Have you ever decided to stop drinking for a week or so, but only lasted for a couple of days?**

⊙ Yes ⊙ No

2 - **Do you wish people would mind their own business about your drinking-- stop telling you what to do?**

⊙ Yes ⊙ No

3 - **Have you ever switched from one kind of drink to another in the hope that this would keep you from getting drunk?**

⊙ Yes ⊙ No

4 - **Have you had to have an eye-opener upon awakening during the past year?**

⊙ Yes ⊙ No

by the Fellowship of Recovering Lutheran Clergy

5 - Do you envy people who can drink without getting into trouble?

○ Yes ○ No

6 - Have you had problems connected with drinking during the past year?

○ Yes ○ No

7 - Has your drinking caused trouble at home?

○ Yes ○ No

8 - Do you ever try to get "extra" drinks at a party because you do not get enough?

○ Yes ○ No

9 - Do you tell yourself you can stop drinking any time you want to, even though you keep getting drunk when you don't mean to?

○ Yes ○ No

10 - Have you missed days of work or school because of drinking?

○ Yes ○ No

11 - Do you have "blackouts"?

○ Yes ○ No

Our Stories of Experience, Strength, & Hope

12 - Have you ever felt that your life would be better if you did not drink?

○ Yes ○ No

What's your score?

Bottom of Form

Did you answer **YES** four or more times? If so, you are probably in trouble with alcohol. Why do we say this? Because thousands of people in A.A. have said so for many years. They found out the truth about themselves — the hard way.

But again, only *you* can decide whether you think A.A. is for you. Try to keep an open mind on the subject. If the answer is **YES**, we will be glad to show you how we stopped drinking ourselves. Just call the FRLC: 1 800 528-0842.

The FRLC does not promise to solve your life's problems. But we can show you how we are learning to live without drinking "one day at a time." We stay away from that "first drink." If there is no first one, there cannot be a tenth one. And when we got rid of alcohol, we found that life became much more manageable.

Addiction Assessment

Check the **YES** box next to any symptoms that you may be experiencing. The term "Using" refers to anything you may be addicted to—drugs, work, food, pornography, sex, gambling, the internet, you name it.

DO YOU LOSE TIME FROM WORK DUE TO USING? ○ Yes ○ No

IS USING MAKING YOUR HOME LIFE UNHAPPY? ○ Yes ○ No

HAVE YOU EVER FELT REMORSE AFTER USING? ○ Yes ○ No

HAVE YOU GOTTEN INTO FINANCIAL DIFFICULTIES AS A RESULT OF USING? ○ Yes ○ No

DOES YOUR USING MAKE YOU CARELESS OF YOUR FAMILY'S WELFARE? ○ Yes ○ No

DO YOU CRAVE USING AT A DEFINITE TIME DAILY? ○ Yes ○ No

Our Stories of Experience, Strength, & Hope

DO YOU WANT TO USE THE NEXT MORNING? ○ Yes ○ No

ARE YOU EXPERIENCING DECREASED ENERGY, INSOMNIA, OR CHANGES IN DIET AS A RESULT OF USING? ○ Yes ○ No

HAVE YOU EVER HAD A COMPLETE LOSS OF MEMORY AS A RESULT OF USING? ○ Yes ○ No

DO YOU USE TO ESCAPE FROM WORRIES OR PROBLEMS. ○ Yes ○ No

Did you answer **YES** four or more times? If so, you are probably in trouble with addiction.

We will be glad to show you what do to. Just call the FRLC: 1 800 528-0842.

The FRLC does not promise to solve your life's problems. But we can show you how we are learning to recover from addiction "one day at a time."

Top of Form

Bottom of Form

Codependency

Characteristics of Co-Dependent People Are: (Any pastors fit these descriptions?)

- An exaggerated sense of responsibility for the actions of others.
- A tendency to confuse love and pity, tendency to "love" people they can pity and rescue.
- A tendency to do more than their share, all of the time.
- A tendency to become hurt when people don't recognize their efforts.
- An unhealthy dependence on relationships. The co-dependent will do anything to hold on to a relationship to avoid the feeling of abandonment.
- An extreme need for approval and recognition.
- A sense of guilt when asserting themselves.
- A compelling need to control others.
- Lack of trust in self and/or others.
- Fear of being abandoned or alone.
- Difficulty identifying feelings.
- Rigidity/difficulty adjusting to change.
- Problems with intimacy/boundaries.

- Chronic anger.
- Lying/dishonesty.
- Poor communication.
- Difficulty making decisions.

Are You Co-Dependent?

This condition appears to run in different degrees, whereby the intensity of symptoms are on a spectrum of severity, as opposed to an all or nothing scale. Please note that only a qualified professional can make a diagnosis of co-dependency; not everyone experiencing these symptoms suffers from co-dependency.

1. Do you keep quiet to avoid arguments?
2. Are you always worried about others' opinions of you?
3. Have you ever lived with someone with an alcohol or drug problem?
4. Have you ever lived with someone who hits or belittles you?
5. Are the opinions of others more important than your own?
6. Do you have difficulty adjusting to changes at work or home?
7. Do you feel rejected when significant others spend time with friends?
8. Do you doubt your ability to be who you want to be?
9. Are you uncomfortable expressing your true feelings to others?
10. Have you ever felt inadequate?

11. Do you feel like a "bad person" when you make a mistake?
12. Do you have difficulty taking compliments or gifts?
13. Do you feel humiliation when your child or spouse makes a mistake?
14. Do you think people in your life would go downhill without your constant efforts?
15. Do you frequently wish someone could help you get things done?
16. Do you have difficulty talking to people in authority, such as the police or your boss?
17. Are you confused about who you are or where you are going with your life?
18. Do you have trouble saying "no" when asked for help?
19. Do you have trouble asking for help?
20. Do you have so many things going at once that you can't do justice to any of them?

Get Help

If you are a member of the clergy and suspect you are struggling with alcohol, addiction in any of its many forms, or codependency (clergy are a high risk population for addiction and codependency), we urge you to get some help—now! Get to an appropriate 12-Step meeting and listen with an open mind. God wants to bring salvation and healing into your life; and God will, if you are willing to humble yourself and say these most difficult words: "I need help." We as recovering clergy are certain about one thing: You cannot do it alone. If you do not ask for help, you will most likely continue to suffer. But if you ask for help, God will give you more than you need. It is a humbling, but powerful experience.

"My grace is sufficient for you, for my power is made perfect in weakness." 2 Cor. 12:9

We found great miracles beginning to happen in our lives after reaching out for help. We found health, healing and salvation—new life!

If you are still unsure and want more information, call the FRLC. We will be glad to assist you. We are a completely independent, not affiliated, non-profit organization made up solely of ELCA and LCMS Lutheran clergy recovering from alcoholism,

Our Stories of Experience, Strength, & Hope

addiction, and codependency. We have no dues or fees and are completely self-supporting through our own contributions. We promise your anonymity and privacy are strictly protected.

You may call for help or more information at:

800-528-0842

or email us at:

New-Life@att.net

A recovering pastor will answer the phone, or you will be given a recorded list of numbers to call for help.

There is hope for you. You are not alone. Ask for help.

For Bishops, District Presidents and Synod Councils

We as a fellowship recommend to the institutional church the following policy as an effective program for supporting clergy through the process of recovery. We suggest you take this policy before your governing bodies and vote on it as your standard practice for dealing with those recovering from alcoholism, addiction and co-dependency.

PROPOSED SYNOD/DISTRICT IMPAIRED PROFESSIONALS POLICY FOR LUTHERAN CLERGY

Rationale: Impaired Professionals policies are currently in place among airline pilots, medical, dental, pharmaceutical, nursing and legal professionals. These policies have been successfully implemented for many years.

The following proposal is based on programs (*or policies*) that are currently in place for impaired professionals in each of the above professions. These programs (*or policies*) recognize the importance of addressing addiction, mental illness and other chronic disorders in such a manner that the person(s) involved receive appropriate initial treatment and have a structured support system for the first two years following that treatment. The above professions report that an ongoing support results in significantly higher recovery than was the case prior to the initiation of the policy.

Adopting such a policy as a part of a Synod/District structure alleviates the need for direct staff oversight of therapeutic issues by transferring this oversight to professionals with employee assistance or addiction certification credentials. This impaired professionals policy supports appropriate interaction between the Employee Assistance Program (EAP) or treatment program and a designated Synod/District staff person. This policy provides the mechanism for informing Synod/District staff about the progress of the impaired professional insofar as that progress affects the professional's work performance. At the same time, the policy maintains the confidentiality of all the impaired professional's personal issues.

The goal is for the Synod/District to offer maximum support to the impaired professional in

by the Fellowship of Recovering Lutheran Clergy

establishing a healthy personal and professional lifestyle through which all persons involved benefit.

Purpose: The purpose of a Synod/District Impaired Professionals Policy is to provide guidelines for oversight of religious professionals whose addictive/dysfunctional behavior has created problems for themselves and others personally and professionally. The policy is a serious and caring attempt to conserve the investment the Church makes in its professionals. This policy supports three outcomes:

1) The restoration of the impaired professional to appropriate work levels and functions.

2) The assisting of that professional in personal healing.

3) The reconciliation of him/her with all whom may have been affected.

Guidelines: When the Synod/District suspects that a substance abuse problem, mental illness or other personal problem is impairing a professional workers' ability to perform his/her function, then the Synod/District will require the professional to have an appropriate evaluation

Our Stories of Experience, Strength, & Hope

by properly credentialed professionals or agencies who meet with the approval of the District/Synod.

The impaired professional may seek a second opinion but such an opinion must also be someone the District/Synod deems appropriate. The District/Synod will require that the impaired professional sign a release of information for only two purposes:

1) So that the District/Synod will have the recommendations of the evaluation.
2) So that the District/Synod may determine the impaired professional's fitness for duty.

The District/Synod may determine that carrying out the recommendations of the evaluation is a condition of continued employment.

For impaired professionals who have chronic disease such as mental illnesses, chemical dependency or other identifiable addictions, the District/Synod will monitor the impaired professional's progress for two years following treatment.

For impaired professionals with chemical dependency or other addictions such progress will include carrying out the recommendations of the EAP or addictions

by the Fellowship of Recovering Lutheran Clergy
professionals for two years. These recommendations will include:

1) Active involvement in an appropriate Twelve-Step or other appropriate support group. Active involvement includes obtaining a sponsor and frequent attendance at group meetings.
2) Individual and/or group therapy on a regular basis with a properly credentialed professional for a period of two (2) years.

Monitoring the progress of the impaired professional will include the following:

1) The synod/district will maintain regular contact with the counseling agency or other therapeutic professional throughout this two-year period. Such contact may be as often as once a week or as infrequent as once a quarter, depending on the particular circumstances.
2) The Synod/District staff person will also maintain regular contact with the EAP for the purposes of continuing to determine the impaired professional's fitness for duty and to determine if the impaired professional is carrying out the terms of the treatment and recovery program.

Our Stories of Experience, Strength, & Hope

If the impaired professional fails to carry out any element of the prescribed recovery program in the two-year period, then Synod/District officials will determine employment status in consultation with the EAP or other therapeutic professional.

The Synod/District will also encourage family members to become involved in an appropriate counseling process and recovery group, inasmuch as they have been affected by/contributed to the problem.

About The Author

A collection of stories about Lutheran clergy who were addicted/alcoholic/codependent and found new life in recovery. Modeled after the book "Alcoholics Anonymous."

Printed in the United States
26663LVS00001B/88-312